MYRA STREET

C L A S S I C

Fish Dishes

MYRA STREET

CLASSIC

Fish Dishes

CHARTWELL
BOOKS, INC.

A QUINTET BOOK

Published by Chartwell Books Inc.,
A Division of Book Sales Inc.,
110 Enterprise Avenue,
Secaucus, New Jersey 07094

ISBN 0-89009-857-3

This book was designed and produced by
Quintet Publishing Limited
6 Blundell Street, London N7

Art design by Bridgewater Associates
Editor Cheen Horn
Photographer John Heseltine

Typeset in Great Britain by
Q.V. Typesetting Limited, London
Color origination in Hong Kong by
Universal Colour Scanning Limited
Printed in Hong Kong by Leefung-Asco
Printers Limited

Contents

Introduction

Baked fish

INTRODUCTION

It is always fascinating to see that many people will eat fish dishes in restaurants, yet rarely will they prepare the same simple fare at home. Fish is very often best cooked without frills, by grilling, baking or poaching, and no one does more preparation for the consumer than the fish shop! There is very little waste as the bones and heads can be used to make fish stock. It is often the thought of making these stocks which makes fish cookery seem complicated. In fact, they are the work of minutes and greatly enhance the delicate flavour of the fish when cooked; it is generally much quicker to cook fish than meat.

Nowadays there is such a variety of fish available that the choice can be bewildering and many cooks tend to stick to the familiar few. But with a little experiment, great variety can be added to everyday menus. Excellent freezing techniques have made it possible to buy a great selection. Fish is often frozen at sea and therefore extremely fresh if properly stored and thawed.

More expensive fish such as salmon, turbot and halibut are excellent value for money because, being rich, large portions are unnecessary. Shellfish are extremely versatile, highly nutritious and amazingly simple to prepare if you are a novice fish cook. Ask your fish shop for advice and they will usually do all the groundwork for you.

Fish is an excellent source of protein and, as most people are conscious of healthy eating, it is comforting to know that the fat content of fish is highly unsaturated. This means fish, as long as it is not fried, can play a valuable part in providing the protein we need without adding to the cholesterol levels associated with heart disease.

The nutrient content of most fish is made up as follows: 25% protein; 22% fats; 2% minerals and 85% water. White fish have very little fat in the flesh, about 0.5%, and in some fish such as haddock or cod, the fat is laid down in the liver. This makes the flesh of white fish particularly valuable in low fat diets. Because the fat is mainly unsaturated, even the oily fish, such as mackerel and herring, are wonderful sources of high-energy food. Recent research suggests that fish oils can help to break down cholesterol in the body. Fish and fish oils are a rich source of vitamins A and D which we all need for glowing health.

The ideal slimmer's food usually contains very little carbohydrate and this makes fish suitable for diets. However, calorie counters must sacrifice all those delicious buttery sauces and settle instead for poaching and baking with the addition of lemon juice and fresh herbs. Mind you, this is not such a sacrifice for the end result will be just as tasty. Those on gluten-free and diabetic diets can also enjoy fish providing that no flour products are used in their preparation.

The fish used for recipes in this book are often interchangeable with other similar types of fish. Although classic recipes may seem forbidding, I have simplified where possible and have included many popular favourites which are becoming 'little classics', especially in the section for appetizers.

Fish appetizers are so popular now for entertaining that fish as a main course is often overlooked, which is a pity. Fish can be ideal as a party main course or the focus of the buffet table. Its delicacy should always be remembered when choosing vegetables and wine. Strong flavours can spoil the taste of the fish.

SELECTION OF FISH

Tomatoes, mushrooms, peas, French beans, broccoli, carrots, leeks and potatoes are all good basic vegetables to serve. Rice with onion, chopped tomato and chopped pepper is delicious too with fish dishes which have a sauce, but rice and fish without a sauce can be rather dry and uninteresting.

The sauce section in the book is important, as many simple dishes have classic sauces served with them and it is these which turn the meal into a feast.

Fish is nutritious and priced competitively in comparison with other high-protein foods, and enables you to produce gourmet meals quickly. There is no reason for people to feel unsure of their abilities to cook any variety of fish dishes. Make a decision today to include more fish dishes in your menus and you will be delighted with the results.

SELECTION

When buying fish and shellfish absolute freshness is essential. Bright eyes and stiff flesh are the signs of fresh fish. Dull eyes and limp flesh with a slight ammonia smell indicate stale fish.

It is best to buy fish the day it is to be cooked. Store it in the refrigerator loosely covered and try not to keep it longer than 24 hours before cooking.

PREPARATION OF FISH

PREPARATION OF FISH

Ideally, fish should be prepared just before cooking but time does not always permit this. If it is to be cooked in a stock it is often advantageous to allow it to cool in the fish liquid.

Most people are not keen on cleaning or gutting fish and it is fortunate that fish shops are so helpful with preparation. However, for those who are prepared to do the work themselves, this is how it should be done.

To scale fish. Lay fish on a piece of kitchen paper and hold by the tail. Scrape scales always from the tail towards the head using the blunt side of a knife. Rinse under cold water.

TO CLEAN AND FILLET FLAT FISH

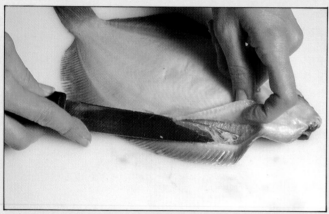

Slit behind the head on the dark skin side, remove the entrails from the cavity and rinse in cold water. Pat dry with a clean cloth or kitchen paper. Remove the fins with a sharp knife or scissors.
1 Begin filleting the fish by cutting into head end against the bone.

2 Cut the fillet away carefully with the skin attached to it, leaving the bone as clean as possible.

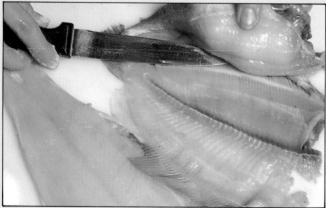

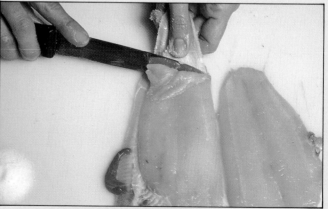

3 Turn the fish over, insert the knife at the head and carefully remove the second fillet in the same way. The flat fish is now filleted. One fillet has thick black skin, the other white skin. The bone can now be used for fish stock (see p 18)

4 To skin the fish, hold the tail firmly and work fillet away from the skin from tail to head, with a sharp knife. The skin can also be used for fish stock.

PREPARATION OF FISH

TO CLEAN AND BONE ROUND FISH

1 If the head is not required as with, for example, mackerel and herring, cut it off with a sharp knife before boning.

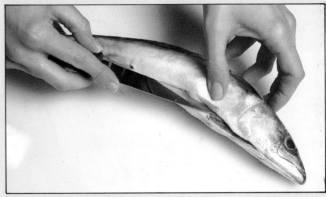

2 To clean, retaining the head, slit from under the head down to the tail.

3 Remove entrails by hooking the finger under the throat and pulling down towards the tail. Wash well. A rubber glove may be used for this step.

4 Slip the sharp knife under the bone on each side of the fish in turn, open and remove bone.

5 An alternative method which may be easier for the inexperienced is to turn the fish open side downwards. Press down on the back with the heel of the hand to loosen the bone.

6 Turn the fish over and starting at the tail end, place the blade of the knife under the bone and push along the spine to release. Feel the surface of the fish with the fingers to ensure there are no stray bones. The round fish is now ready to be cooked.

BAKING

This method of cookery uses a controlled temperature in an oven. When fat or oil is used the food is said to be roasted. Baking in the oven is suitable for whole fish and fish fillets.

1 Foil and casseroles are often used for baking fish. Baking ensures an even distribution of heat for the complete cooking of fish, or the first stage of a fish dish, which may have a delicious sauce made from the juices left over from the cooking in the oven.

2 Most whole fish are baked at *180°C/350°F/Gas 4* .

3 Smaller fish or fillets are usually cooked at around *200°C/400°F/Gas 6* for a shorter time (see individual recipes).

4 Fish should be brushed with a little fat or oil, and usually some liquid such as Court-Bouillon (see p 19) or wine flavoured with herbs is added.

BRAISING OR CASSEROLING

This method can be carried out either on top of the stove or in the oven and will include a selection of vegetables, stock or wine with the fish which is cooked in a casserole or ovenproof dish.

1 Remember that the vegetables must be tender at the same time as the fish is cooked. Therefore, it is usually advisable to sweat the vegetables first (by cooking over a low heat) to make sure that they are partially cooked before adding the fish.

2 Large chunks of fish, fish steaks or cutlets can be cooked by this method.

METHODS OF COOKING FISH

MICROWAVE COOKING

The microwave oven cooks fish very successfully, retaining all the natural moisture and delicacy. It is also an excellent way to reheat dishes to avoid any loss of texture and flavour.

1 Usually it is advisable to cook covered with plastic wrap clingfilm which has had slits cut.

2 Place the thinner ends of the fish towards the middle of the dish and these can be overlapped if necessary.

3 To cook fish which requires flaking in the recipe, cook until just firm then allow to stand for a few minutes. It will then flake easily.

4 Brush fish such as trout which has the skin left on with butter, otherwise no fat is necessary.

5 If sauce is to be added to the fish in the microwave, it is usually advisable to do this halfway through the cooking process.

6 Cooking fish fillets takes approximately 9 – 10 minutes per lb at 500 watts; 7 – 8 minutes per lb at 600 watts; 6 – 7 minutes per lb at 650 watts.

Whole fish will take approximately 11 – 13 minutes per lb at 500 watts; 8 – 10 minutes per lb at 600 watts; 7 – 9 minutes per lb at 650 watts.

DEEP FRYING

Although many people try to cut down on fried food, this is one of the most traditional and delicious ways to eat some fish. It is especially suited to small fish, such as whitebait, sprats and fish fillets, and it is a popular way to cook scampi.

1 Food must be coated before frying to provide a crisp outside and to prevent the fish breaking up and the fat soaking through.

2 Pre-heat the fat to *170° – 190°C / 325 – 375°F,* depending on the size of the fish. It is essential to have hot oil to seal the coating and prevent soggy oily fish.

3 To test for correct frying temperature without a thermostat use a cube of stale bread: drop into the fat and it should rise to the surface crisp and evenly browned in 1 minute if the temperature is correct.

4 There are many safe and useful electric friers on the market with temperature controls which remove the guesswork from frying.

5 If using a deep fat frying pan with a basket, care must be taken to avoid accidents. The pan should be filled to less than two-thirds full. Do not allow naked flames to lick up the sides of the pan. Should an accident occur and the fat catch fire, do not use water to douse the flames, but cover immediately with a metal lid to exclude the air and turn off the heat immediately. Try not to lift the pan.

METHODS OF COOKING FISH

STEAMING

This method of cooking fish makes it light and easy to digest. It is an excellent way to cook food for babies, convalescents and anyone with a digestive problem, or who is on a light diet.
1 Fillets can be rolled or pieces placed between two plates over steadily simmering water. Otherwise use a steaming saucepan or a pressure cooker.
2 With the pressure cooker follow the manufacturers directions for best results.

POACHING

This method involves cooking, usually whole fish fillets and steaks, gently in liquid.
1 Place the liquid in a frying pan or saucepan as large as the fish.
2 Milk, stock, water or wine can all be used according to the recipe, usually with herbs and seasonings. Place the prepared fish in the pan; whole fillets such as smoked haddock can be topped with small knobs of butter.
3 Poaching is done over a low heat. If the liquid is allowed to boil, the fish will lose its delicate taste and texture. The liquor left over from poaching can be used as liquid for a sauce to accompany the fish.

METHODS OF COOKING FISH

GRILLING (BROILING)

A fast method of cooking fillets of fish, fish steaks, cutlets and small whole fish. To save extra washing up it is advisable to line the grill pan (broiler) with foil, and to prevent the fish sticking to the wire rack, brush with oil before starting to cook.

1 Pre-heat the grill and brush the fish with melted butter or oil. Whole fish should have several cuts made in the skin to allow the heat to penetrate evenly.

2 Season and place the fish under the grill. After 1 minute, lower heat to medium. Most average-sized fish or cutlets will take about 8 – 10 minutes.

EN PAPILLOTE

This means cooking food in a paper case in the oven. It is especially good for whole fish and steaks as all the goodness and flavour are sealed in the parcel. The added advantage is that there is no messy pan to clean.

1 The fish can be enclosed in a buttered piece of waxed greaseproof paper though most people use foil for 'parcel' cooking now.

2 It is an ideal method of cooking for slimmers as the fish is simply sprinkled with lemon juice, herbs and seasoning and cooked in its own juice.

SHALLOW FRYING

Shallow frying, which is sometimes known as sautéing, covers the method of cooking the fish in a frying pan in a shallow layer of oil or fat.

1 Coat the food in either flour or egg and crumbs, as in deep frying.

2 The food will require turning and looking after constantly to obtain an overall even golden-brown and crisp appearance.

Sauces

Béchamel Sauce *18*

Court-Bouillon *19*

Mornay Sauce *20*

Hollandaise Sauce *21*

Béarnaise Sauce *21*

Mousseline Sauce *21*

Mayonnaise *22*

Aïoli *22*

Sauce Gribiche *22*

Green Sauce *23*

Seafood Sauce *23*

Tartare Sauce *24*

Spicy Tomato Sauce *27*

Tomato Sauce *28*

Mustard Sauce *29*

Maître D'Hôtel Butter *30*

Green Butter *30*

Garlic Butter *31*

Anchovy Butter *31*

Mustard Butter *31*

Lemon Tarragon Butter *31*

A most important ingredient in excellent fish dishes is very often the accompanying sauce or the sauce in which the fish is cooked. These sauces and stocks appear again and again in fish dishes and are worth mastering.

BÉCHAMEL SAUCE

A good béchamel enhances any dish requiring a white sauce and is well worth the extra few minutes it takes to prepare.

Makes 2½ cups / 600 ml / 1 pt sauce
2½ cups / 600 ml / 1 pt milk
1 small peeled onion, quartered
1 bay leaf
a few peppercorns
1 blade of mace
1 stalk parsley
6–7 tbsp / 50 g / 1½ – 1¾ oz butter, depending on thickness required
3 – 3½ tbsp / 50 g / 1½ – 1¾ oz flour, depending on thickness required
salt and white pepper

1 Place the milk in a saucepan with the onion, bay leaf, peppercorns, mace and parsley. Cover and allow to heat up on a low heat for about 10 minutes without boiling. Remove from the heat and allow to stand for a further 10 minutes covered. Strain and set aside.

2 Make the roux (a liaison of butter and flour) by melting the butter in a saucepan — do not allow to brown. Add the flour and mix well over a low heat.

3 Gradually add the strained milk and continue stirring until creamy and thick, season to taste.

In some fish dishes half or all of the milk is substituted by using the liquid in which the fish has been baked or poached.

Sauce made with a stock or stock and wine is known as a velouté sauce.

FISH STOCK

To make a good fish stock, add fish trimmings to the Court-Bouillon opposite leaving out the vinegar. The vegetables should not be simmered for longer than 30 minutes, or the stock will become bitter.

Note After fish has been cooked in the Court-Bouillon, the liquid becomes a fish stock.

COURT-BOUILLON

Used for cooking salmon, trout, crawfish and lobster

To cook 3 kg / 6 lb fish
10 cups / 2 1/4 pt water
2 tsp salt
2 cups / 225 g / 8 oz carrots, peeled and sliced
2 cups / 225 g / 8 oz onions, peeled and sliced
¼ cup / 25 g / 1 oz parsley stalks
4 tbsp white wine or white wine vinegar
2 bouquets garnis or 2 bay leaves
sprigs of thyme
6 slightly crushed peppercorns

1 Place all the ingredients except the peppercorns in a fish kettle or large saucepan. Bring the liquid to the boil and skim.

2 Simmer for approximately 3–5 minutes then add the crushed peppercorns, continue simmering for a further 10–20 minutes. Allow to cool and strain through a fine sieve.

3 Use as required. After cooking fish in the court-bouillon the stock can be used several times if strained each time.

To store, pour into a plastic bag set in bowl or plastic box and freeze until cooking fish again.

The bag may be taken out when frozen and sealed. This quantity is for large fish (weighing about 3 kg/6 lb) and may be halved for smaller quantities.

MORNAY SAUCE

Makes approximately 2½ cups / 600 ml / 1 pt
2½ cups / 600 ml / 1 pt béchamel sauce
2 egg yolks
4 tbsp cream
½ cup / 50 g / 2 oz grated cheese

1 Place 4 tbsp béchamel sauce in a small bowl and mix with the egg yolks and cream.

2 Add this mixture to the béchamel sauce and cook over a low heat, stirring well.

3 Gradually add grated cheese. Parmesan is ideal but individual taste can decide on the type of cheese.

Can be served with poached or steamed fillets or cutlets.

CHAUDFROID SAUCE

Makes 2½ cups / 600 ml / 1 pt
2 cups / 450 ml / ¾ pt béchamel sauce
⅝ cup / 150 ml / ¼ pt aspic jelly
1 rounded tsp gelatine
2 tbsp boiling water

1 Allow the bechamel sauce to cool but cover with plastic wrap clingfilm to avoid a skin forming.

2 Make up the aspic jelly in a jug and sprinkle the gelatine onto the hot water. Make sure the mixture is dissolved by placing the jug in a saucepan of boiling water. Allow to cool before using to coat fish fillets, small fish or steaks.

MORNAY SAUCES

Makes 1¾ cups / 300 ml / ½ pt
¾ cup / 175 g / 6 oz butter
2 tbsp water
6 slightly crushed peppercorns
1 tbsp white wine vinegar
2 egg yolks
1 tbsp lemon juice
salt to taste

1 Make the sauce in a double boiler or an ovenproof bowl over a saucepan of hot water. If using the latter method make sure that the bottom of the bowl is not touching the hot water or the sauce will set on the bottom of the bowl before it is cooked.

2 Place the water, crushed peppercorns and white wine vinegar in a small saucepan and reduce to about 1 tbsp liquid. Set aside.

3 Cut the butter into pieces and soften gently in a small saucepan. Remove from heat.

4 Whisk the egg yolks, reduced liquid and a little of the butter in the double boiler. When the mixture becomes creamy and slightly thick, pour in the butter in a thin stream, whisking briskly. Add lemon juice and a little salt, and taste for seasoning.

5 Remove from the heat immediately it is thick. Should the sauce look as if it is curdling, add a few drops of cold water and whisk briskly for a few more minutes. This sauce can be made in a blender or food processor, but you may find that less butter will be absorbed. The addition of 1 tbsp cold water with the lemon juice will prevent it becoming too thick.

Hollandaise is served hot with grilled (broiled) fish such as salmon, turbot, halibut and sea bream.

BEARNAISE SAUCE

Add another teaspoon of vinegar and some tarragon to the ingredients in step 2 for Hollandaise Sauce before reducing. The flavour of béarnaise is altogether more piquant and the end result should be slightly thicker than hollandaise with 1 tbsp chopped tarragon and 1 tbsp chopped chervil added. If these are unobtainable, use 2 tsp dried tarragon and 1 tbsp fresh chopped parsley.

MOUSSELINE SAUCE

Add 4 tbsp whipped cream to the Hollandaise Sauce as it cools and the resulting mousseline sauce can be served cold with fish or vegetables.

Makes approximately 1¼ cups / 300 ml / ½ pt
2 egg yolks
1¼ cups / 300 ml / ½ pt vegetable or olive oil
½ tsp salt
pinch of white pepper
pinch of dried mustard
1 tbsp white wine vinegar or lemon juice

1 Use the eggs at room temperature, not directly from the refrigerator. Place the yolks in a *slightly* warmed but dry bowl. Mix yolks for a few seconds.

2 Gradually add the oil a few drops at a time, beating constantly with a wooden spoon or a small wire whisk. The mixture will become a thick creamy emulsion after a little oil is added. Continue to beat in the rest of the oil gradually.

3 Mix the rest of the ingredients together and add a few drops at a time when the mixture becomes thick; this will make the sauce thinner. Taste for seasoning.

AIOLI

Soak 1 slice of bread in a little milk, or use 1 small mashed potato.

Crush 2–4 cloves of garlic depending on taste and mix with the squeezed bread or potato. Make a paste, then add only one egg yolk to the mixture.

Proceed as for Mayonnaise but add 1–2 tbsp boiled warm water when the mixture becomes thick.

Serve with grilled (broiled) and cold fish and shellfish. It is also served with Provencal fish soups.

SAUCE GRIBICHE

Add the sieved yolk of a hard-boiled (hard-cooked) egg, ½ tsp Dijon mustard, 1 tbsp chopped gherkins, 1 tsp fresh tarragon or ½ tsp dried, 1 tbsp freshly chopped parsley and 1 tsp chopped capers to 1¼ cups / 300 ml / ½ pt mayonnaise. The egg white cut into very thin strips may be added before serving. Serve with cold fish dishes and shellfish.

SAUCES

GREEN SAUCE

Liquidize 1 bunch of washed watercress with stalks removed with 2 tbsp/50 g/2 oz cooked and well drained fresh or frozen spinach, a few sprigs of parsley, 2 tsp fresh tarragon or 1 tsp dried, and add to the Mayonnaise. Delicious served with cold fish dishes.

SEAFOOD SAUCE

Add ⅝ cup/150 ml/¼ pt whipped cream with 2 tsp brandy added and a few drops of tabasco sauce to 1¼ cups/300 ml/½ pt well flavoured mayonnaise.

Note All these sauces can be made in a blender or food processor. I always use the whole egg when making this type of sauce in a machine. The advantage is that the machine produces a finer emulsion which keeps longer than the hand-made variety, and only takes a few seconds to make.

If using chilled mayonnaise-type sauces, allow them to return to room temperature before stirring to avoid separation.

To rescue what is commonly known as 'curdled mayonnaise' (this can happen if the oil is added too fast or the ingredients are too cold), start again with another egg yolk, a pinch of mustard and a few drops of hot water. Put the mixture in a clean warm bowl and add the curdled sauce, one spoonful at a time, whisking briskly. When the sauce becomes an emulsion again, add the remainder of the curdled sauce gradually, whisking until a thick creamy mixture is made. Taste for seasoning.

Grilled sardines with green sauce

TARTARE SAUCE

Makes 1¼ cups / 300 ml / ½ pt
2 hard-boiled (hard-cooked) eggs
2 tsp French mustard
salt and freshly ground pepper
1 egg yolk
⅝ cup / 150 ml / ¼ pt vegetable or olive oil
4–6 gherkins
2 tbsp capers
2 tbsp parsley, finely chopped
1 tsp dried chervil or fresh if available

This sauce recipe is not suitable for the blender.

1 Sieve the yolks of the hard-boiled eggs into a bowl and add mustard, salt and pepper.

2 Mix the raw egg yolk into the bowl and cream until the mixture is a smooth paste.

3 Add the oil a few drops at a time until the sauce is thick. If it seems too thick add a few drops of lemon juice.

4 Drain and rinse the gherkins and capers in a sieve under the cold tap as they are usually packed in vinegar or brine, which can overpower the flavour of the sauce. Pat dry with kitchen towels and chop finely.

5 Add to the sauce with the herbs (herbs, gherkins and capers can be chopped in the blender or food processor). Mix well and taste for seasoning. Serve with all types of fried or grilled (broiled) fish.

QUICK TARTARE SAUCE

Add the gherkins, capers, parsley and herbs to ⅝ cup / 150 ml / ¼ pt mayonnaise.

SPICY TOMATO SAUCE

Makes 2 cups / 450 ml / ¾ pt
2 tbsp oil
1 large onion, peeled and chopped
1 green pepper, deseeded
1 red pepper, deseeded
1 hot pepper, deseeded and finely chopped
1½ cups/1 × 400 g/14-oz can of tomatoes
2 fresh tomatoes, skinned and chopped
¼ tsp dried mustard
salt and freshly ground pepper
1 bouquet garni
2 bay leaves
¼ tsp sugar
⅝ cup / 150 ml / ¼ pt fish or chicken stock
To garnish
1 green chilli, deseeded and finely chopped

1 Heat the oil in a saucepan and sweat the onion on a low heat until transparent.

2 Dice the peppers finely. Add with the chilli to the onions and cook on a low heat for about 4 minutes.

3 Add the rest of the ingredients to the onion and pepper mixture. Bring to the boil, reduce the heat and simmer for 30 minutes.

4 Remove bouquet garni and bay leaves.

5 The sauce may be partially blended if liked. Serve with chopped green chilli on top.

T O M A T O   S A U C E

Makes approximately 2½ cups / 600 ml / 1 pt
2 tbsp oil
1 large onion, peeled and diced
1–2 cloves garlic, crushed
1 stalk celery, scrubbed
1 carrot, scraped and grated
1½ cups / 1 × 400-g / 14-oz can tomatoes
1½ cups / 450 g / 1 lb fresh tomatoes, skinned and chopped
1 bouquet garni
2 bay leaves
1 tbsp chopped fresh basil, or 1 tsp dried basil
1 tsp dried basil
parsley sprig
½ tsp sugar
salt and freshly ground black pepper
1¼ cups / 300 ml / ½ pt fish or chicken stock
2 tbsp red wine

1 Heat the oil in a saucepan. Cook the garlic and onions over a low heat for about 4 minutes until transparent.

2 Remove the strings from the celery stalk and chop into small pieces, then add to the onion and garlic for the last 2 minutes.

3 Add all the other ingredients, bring to the boil and simmer for 40 minutes on a low heat.

4 Remove the sprig of parsley, bay leaf and bouquet garni and serve as cooked, or the sauce may be partially blended if a smoother texture is preferred.

MUSTARD SAUCE

Makes ⅝ cup / 150 ml / ¼ pt
1 tbsp French mustard
juice of ½ lemon
salt and white pepper
⅝ cup / 150 ml / ¼ pt whipping cream

1 Mix the mustard, lemon juice and seasoning together.

2 Whip the cream lightly and stir in the mustard mixture. Chill before using with grilled or fried fish.

VARIATION

Alternatively a hot mustard sauce may be made with ⅝ cup / 150 ml / ¼ pt Béchamel Sauce (see p 18). Add 1 tsp dried mustard and 1 tsp vinegar to 1 tbsp of the sauce, return to the sauce and stir over the heat for a further minute.

It is usual to make up herb butters in the shape of a round sausage. Wrap the round in foil and cut slices as required after chilling. It is convenient to make up several flavours. Cut the rolls into coin-sized pieces when very cold and store in the freezer.

MAITRE D'HOTEL BUTTER
4 tbsp / 50 g / 2 oz butter
2 tsp lemon juice
salt and freshly ground pepper
1 tbsp chopped parsley

Cream all ingredients together, chill and use on grilled (broiled) food.

GREEN BUTTER
2 tbsp / 50 g / 2 oz spinach leaves, washed
1 bunch of watercress, stalks removed
1 clove of garlic
fresh tarragon to taste
a few sprigs of parsley
fresh chives to taste
3 gherkins
1 tsp capers
3 anchovy fillets
2 tbsp oil
1 egg yolk
1 hard-boiled (hard-cooked) egg
½ cup / 100 g / 4 oz butter

1 It is simple to make this excellent savoury butter in a blender or food processor, otherwise all ingredients have to be chopped by hand.

2 Drop the spinach leaves, watercress, garlic and herbs into the goblet to purée. Add the gherkins, capers and anchovy fillets with the oil, egg yolk and hard-boiled egg. Lastly blend in the softened butter.

Chill and serve with grilled (broiled) fish. This savoury butter is especially good with barbecued food.

GARLIC BUTTER

4 tbsp / 50g / 2 oz butter
1–2 cloves garlic, crushed
2 tsp fresh parsley, chopped

1 Cream the butter and add the well crushed garlic. Blend well. Parsley is optional but gives a better flavour to the butter.

2 Chill well.

ANCHOVY BUTTER

6 anchovy fillets
2 tbsp milk
6 tbsp / 75 g / 3 oz butter
pepper
1 drop tabasco sauce

1 Soak all the anchovy fillets in milk. Mash in a bowl with a wooden spoon until creamy.

2 Cream all ingredients together and chill.

MUSTARD BUTTER

4 tbsp / 50 g / 2 oz butter
1 tbsp French mustard
salt and pepper

Cream all ingredients together and chill.

LEMON TARRAGON BUTTER

4 tbsp / 2 oz butter
juice of ½ lemon
salt and pepper
fresh tarragon or 1 tsp dried

Cream all ingredients together and chill.

Soups and Starters

Mediterranean Fish Soup *34*

Clam Chowder *36*

Fish Chowder *37*

Smoked Salmon Appetizer *39*

Smoked Mackerel Cream *39*

Taramasalata *40*

Fish Pâté *41*

Kipper Pâté *42*

Whitebait *43*

Prawn or Shrimp Cocktail *44*

Avocado with Prawns
or Shrimps in Seafood Sauce *46*

Fish Savouries with Spicy Tomato Sauce *47*

Avocado, Grapefruit and Prawn
or Shrimp Salads *49*

Baked Avocado with Crab *48*

Savoury Sprats *50*

Smoked mackerel cream

*There are many varieties of fish soups from the
Mediterranean countries, but the price of fish is
gradually making these into luxury dishes.
It is as well to simplify a fish soup to make it possible
for most cooks to attempt and guests to be able to eat
it without battling with bones.*

Serves 4
4 tbsp olive or vegetable oil
1 large onion, finely chopped
2 cloves garlic, crushed
2 stalks celery and leaves
3 cups/2 × 400-g/14-oz cans tomatoes or 1½ cups/1 can and 1½ cups/450 g/1 lb fresh tomatoes, skinned
⅝ cup/150 ml/¼ pt white wine
2½ cups/600 ml/1 pt water
225 g/8 oz whiting, haddock or cod, skinned and filleted
1 mackerel, skinned and filleted
¾ cup/100 g/4 oz prawns or shrimps
600 g/1⅓ lb mussels, washed and rinsed
To garnish
chopped parsley

1 Heat the oil and sauté the onion and garlic for a few minutes until transparent.

2 Add celery leaves and chopped tomatoes, wine, water and seasoning. Cook for 15 minutes.

3 Cut the fish into bite-size pieces and add to the soup. Poach gently for about 10 minutes — do not allow to boil.

4 Meanwhile take a little of the soup broth and place the washed mussels in the heated broth in a frying pan. Shake well until mussels open. Add to the soup with the prawns or shrimps and allow to cook together for another 5 minutes.

5 Sprinkle with chopped parsley and serve with warm crusty bread.

CLAM CHOWDER

Serves 4
1–2 dozen clams or 1 can clams
⅝ cup / 150 ml / ¼ pt white wine
1¼ cups / 300 ml / ½ pt water
1 bay leaf
1 bouquet garni
⅔ cup / 100 g / 4 oz bacon
• 2 tbsp / 25 g / 1 oz butter
1 medium onion, diced
2 leeks, washed and chopped
1 green pepper, deseeded, blanched and diced
1 stalk celery, diced
1 small / 100 g / 4 oz potato, diced
salt and freshly ground pepper
few sprigs fresh thyme or ½ tsp dried thyme
4–6 fresh tomatoes, skinned or 1½ cups / 1 × 425-g / 15-oz can tomatoes
1 tbsp chopped parsley
8 plain crackers, crushed

1 Poach the fresh clams for about 5 minutes in the white wine and water with a bay leaf and bouquet garni added. If using canned, poach for 10 minutes.

2 Cut the streaky bacon into small pieces. Melt the butter in a saucepan and add bacon. After about 2 minutes add the onion, leeks, diced pepper, diced celery and diced potato. Sweat the vegetables for about 6 minutes then add the clam liquor with seasoning, thyme and chopped tomatoes. Make liquid up to approximately 1 1/2 pt with water. Bring the soup to the boil, reduce heat and simmer until the vegetables are tender.

3 Add the clams a few minutes before serving.

Serve the chowder sprinkled with crushed crackers and parsley.

FISH CHOWDER

Serves 4
450 g / 1 lb white fish, boned
2 tbsp / 25 g / 1 oz butter
1 large onion, peeled and finely diced
1–2 cloves garlic, peeled and crushed
4 potatoes, peeled and diced
1½ cups / 1 × 400-g / 14-oz can tomatoes
few sprigs of thyme
few sprigs of parsley
1–2 bay leaves or 1 bouquet garni
salt and freshly ground black pepper
pinch of cayenne pepper
1¼ cups / 300 ml / ½ pt hot water
⅝ cup / 150 ml / ¼ pt milk
8 plain crackers, crushed
1 tbsp chopped parsley

Use whiting, haddock or any leftover raw fish.

1 Make sure the fish is boned as far as possible, as most people object to fish bones. Cut into even-sized pieces.

2 Melt the butter and sweat the onion, crushed garlic and diced potatoes for about 5 minutes.

3 Add the can of tomatoes with the herbs and seasoning. Pour in the hot water.

4 Bring to the boil and simmer for about 20 minutes, or until potatoes are cooked. Add the fish for about the last 10 minutes of cooking. Taste for seasoning and make sure all the fish is cooked.

5 Add the milk and stir over a low heat for a few minutes.

6 Place the crackers in the bottom of the soup bowls and pour over the soup. Sprinkle with chopped parsley.

Serve with warm French bread or crispy rolls.

Fish chowder

SMOKED SALMON APPETIZER

Serves 4
125 g / 4 oz smoked salmon pieces
2 tbsp fresh parsley, chopped
freshly ground black pepper
juice of 2 lemons
¼ cup / 25 g / 1 oz cream cheese
2 tbsp double or whipping cream

1 Select a few small pieces of smoked salmon and retain for garnish. Pound, sieve or blend the remainder, then add a good shake of black pepper and lemon juice and mix well.

2 Add the smoked salmon and chopped parsley to the cream cheese and double or whipping cream. Mix well.

3 This mixture can be piped on crackers or toast as canapés decorated with small curls of smoked salmon or served in small ramekins as an appetizer with triangles of toast.

Smoked salmon appetizer

SMOKED MACKEREL CREAM

Serves 4
1 large / 275 g / 10 oz smoked mackerel fillet
juice of 1 lemon
1 clove garlic, crushed
2 tbsp vegetable or olive oil
¼ cup / 25 g / 1 oz cream cheese
2 tbsp parsley, finely chopped
salt and freshly ground pepper
To garnish
1 lemon cut into wedges

1 Remove the skin from the mackerel and check for any bones which may be left. Mash in a bowl with a fork. Sprinkle with the lemon juice.

2 Mix the crushed garlic, oil and cream cheese in a bowl.

3 Gradually add the fish and the parsley. Season well. Serve in small ramekins.
Alternatively feed the ingredients into a food processor and mix for a few seconds.

4 Serve with triangles of brown toast and lemon wedges.

TARAMASALATA

Serves 4–6
225 g / 8 oz smoked cod's roe
3–4 tbsp lemon juice
1 cup / 3 oz / 75 g boiled potato, sieved
1 slice white bread, crustless
1–2 cloves garlic, crushed
3 tbsp olive oil
1–3 tsp cold water
salt and white pepper
To garnish
12 black olives
sprig of parsley

1 Remove the skin from the cod's roe, carefully scooping away all the flesh. Place in a bowl and sprinkle with 2 tbsp of lemon juice. Mix well with a wooden spoon. Add the sieved potato a bit at a time.

2 Steep the slice of bread in cold water and squeeze dry with one hand. Cream into the fish mixture. Add finely crushed garlic and either one or two cloves, according to individual taste.

3 Beat in the oil a few drops at a time, then gradually add cold water until a thick creamy consistency is reached. Season with white pepper and a little salt (cod's roe can be salty, so taste as seasoning progresses). More lemon juice can be added, if needed.

4 Alternatively feed the oil and garlic into a food processor or large blender and gradually add the other ingredients. The taramasalata will be made in a few minutes. Add cold water at the end to achieve the correct creamy consistency.

5 Garnish with black olives and a sprig of parsley and serve with crisp toast or hot pitta bread.

FISH PATE

Serves 6
450 g / 1 lb raw white fish, skinned and boned
salt and white pepper
a pinch of cayenne pepper
juice of ½ lemon
⅝ cup / 150 ml / ¼ pt single (cereal) cream
2 eggs, separated
1 cup / 50 g / 2 oz fresh white breadcrumbs
a little fresh tarragon
½ tsp dried or 1 tbsp fresh parsley, chopped
butter, melted
1 egg white
5 fillets of sole
8 asparagus tips, cooked
Oven temperature 180°C / 350°F / Gas 4

1 Place the raw fish, which can be whiting, haddock or cod, into a blender or food processor. Blend with a little salt and pepper and a pinch of cayenne. Add a few drops of lemon juice.

2 Whisk 2 egg whites until just frothy (not white), mix into the fish mixture. Chill in the refrigerator.

3 Whip the cream and add half of it to the fish mixture for the first stuffing. Leave to chill.

4 Make the second stuffing by mixing the breadcrumbs in a bowl with the egg yolks, herbs and seasoning. Finally, stir in the other half of the cream.

5 Butter generously the sides and bottom of a 450-g / 1-lb loaf tin (pan).

6 Place a fillet of sole in the bottom to line the tin.

7 Coat the sole with a little egg white and place the first stuffing on top of the sole — use about half. Lay another fillet of sole brushed with the egg white on the stuffing and cover with half the second stuffing. Lay on 4 asparagus tips. Cover with another fillet of sole. Continue to layer the remaining stuffing, separating each layer with 1 fillet of sole. Top with the last fillet of sole and cover with a buttered paper or buttered foil.

8 Place in baking tin (pan), half filled with water, and cook for about 1 hour until firm. If serving hot, allow to cool slightly before turning out. Garnish with remaining asparagus.

The pâté can be served cold or hot.

Serves 4

225 g / 8 oz kipper fillets

2 tbsp lemon juice

freshly ground black pepper

4 tbsp / 50 g / 2 oz butter

2 tbsp parsley, finely chopped

1 tbsp single (cereal) cream

To garnish

parsley

lemon twist

1 Remove the skin from the kipper fillets and mash the fish with a fork. Sprinkle with 1 tbsp lemon juice and season with pepper.

2 Cream the butter in a bowl and add the parsley and cream. Gradually blend in the fish. Taste for seasoning and add more lemon juice to taste.

3 Serve on toast or crackers or in a dish garnished with parsley and lemon twists, surrounded by triangles of toast.

Serves 4

650 g / 1½ lb whitebait

¾ cup / 75 g / 3 oz seasoned flour

oil for frying

To garnish

lemon wedges

parsley sprigs

Frying temperature 180°C/350°F/Gas 4

1 Pat the whitebait dry with kitchen paper towels. (It is often sold frozen and when thawed needs to be patted dry.)

2 Toss the fish in seasoned flour.

3 Deep fry in hot oil for a few minutes until golden brown and crisp.

Serve with lemon wedges, parsley sprigs and Tartare Sauce (see p 24). Offer thinly sliced wholewheat bread and butter.

Possibly the most popular fish appetizer in restaurants, but the special seafood sauce makes it worth serving at home.

Serves 4
a few crispy lettuce leaves, preferably iceberg
1½ cups / 225 g / 8 oz prawns or shrimps
1¼ cups / 300 ml / ½ pt Seafood Sauce (see p 23)
To garnish
prawns or shrimps in shells, or 4 lemon twists
4 sprigs of watercress

1 Shred the lettuce and line the bottoms of 4 glass dishes or wine glasses.

2 Mix the prawns or shrimps with the seafood dressing and pile into the glasses.

3 Garnish with whole prawns or shrimps in shells or a twist of lemon and a sprig of watercress.

SEAFOOD COCKTAIL

Mix prawns or shrimps with cooked crab, lobster meat, clams and mussels or sliced scallops and prepare as above.

AVOCADO WITH PRAWNS OR SHRIMPS IN SEAFOOD SAUCE

Serves 4
2 ripe avocados
lemon juice
¾ cup / 125 g / 4 oz peeled prawns
⅝ cup / 125 ml / ¼ pt Seafood Sauce (see p 23)
To garnish
parsley or watercress
4 prawns in their shells

1 Cut the avocados lengthwise with a sharp stainless steel knife and carefully remove the stone. Scoop out some of the flesh from each half and chop into small pieces. Place in a bowl and sprinkle with lemon juice.

2 Add the prawns or shrimps, making sure they are defrosted, and drained if using frozen, to the seafood sauce. Mix well with the chopped avocado and taste for seasoning. Return to the avocado skins.

3 Garnish with watercress or parsley. Add one or two prawns or shrimps in shells at the narrow end of the avocado half if liked.

FISH SAVOURIES WITH SPICY TOMATO SAUCE

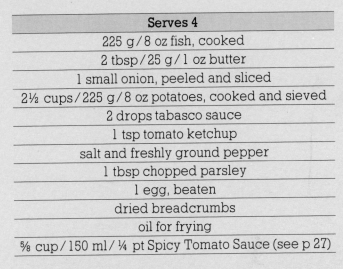

Serves 4
225 g / 8 oz fish, cooked
2 tbsp / 25 g / 1 oz butter
1 small onion, peeled and sliced
2½ cups / 225 g / 8 oz potatoes, cooked and sieved
2 drops tabasco sauce
1 tsp tomato ketchup
salt and freshly ground pepper
1 tbsp chopped parsley
1 egg, beaten
dried breadcrumbs
oil for frying
⅝ cup / 150 ml / ¼ pt Spicy Tomato Sauce (see p 27)

Leftover poached salmon, trout or canned fish such as tuna or salmon can be used.

1 Make sure that all the bones are removed from the cooked fish.

2 Melt the butter and sweat the onion until tender. Add the potatoes, seasoning and parsley to the onion in a bowl, and finally add the fish and mix well.

3 Mix with a little of the beaten egg. Add a few drops of water to the remaining egg. Flour the hands and form the mixture into small balls and chill in the refrigerator.

4 Roll the fish balls in the egg and water mixture, and then in the dried crumbs.

5 Fry the balls in deep fat or in a frying pan one-third filled with oil which has been heated.

6 Serve on a plate. Spear the balls with wooden cocktail sticks or toothpicks and serve around a dish of hot spicy tomato sauce. Can be served with drinks or at buffet parties.

BAKED AVOCADO WITH CRAB

Serves 4
2 ripe avocados
200-g / 7-oz can of crab meat or the meat from 1 cooked crab
1 tbsp lemon juice
2 tbsp white wine
few drops of tabasco sauce
2 tsp tomato purée (paste)
salt and freshly ground pepper
1¼ cups / 300 ml / ½ pt Béchamel Sauce (see p 18)
To garnish
1 tbsp parsley, finely chopped
Oven temperature 180°C / 350°F / Gas 4

1 Cut the avocados in half carefully and remove the stones and some of the flesh.

2 Sprinkle the crab meat and chopped avocado flesh with lemon juice and white wine.

3 Add the rest of the ingredients to the béchamel sauce and fill the halved avocados, piling the mixture up as high as it will go without spilling.

4 Bake in a moderate oven until golden brown. Serve sprinkled with chopped parsley.

This dish can be made with tuna fish in place of crab.

AVOCADO, GRAPEFRUIT AND PRAWN OR SHRIMP SALAD

Serves 4
2 grapefruit
2 avocados
1½ cups / 225 g / 8 oz prawns or shrimps
⅝ cup / 150 ml / ¼ pt French dressing or Seafood Sauce (see p 23)

1 To make the grapefruit sections, place the fruit in a bowl and pour boiling water on top to cover. Leave for 2 minutes, then remove and allow to cool. Cut a slice from the top of the fruit, then cut the peel and pith off in strips to reveal the flesh. It is essential to use a small sharp knife.

2 When all the pith has been cut away, remove each section by cutting between the membranes of each segment. At the end only the tough outer skin should be left and each section of fruit is separate without skin.

3 Peel the avocados, cut in half lengthways and remove the stones. Cut the flesh into slices.

4 Arrange the avocado slices, grapefruit segments and prawns or shrimps in dishes and serve with French dressing, Seafood Sauce or Mayonnaise (see pp 22, 23) as preferred. The dressing may be poured over the salad or served separately.

SAVOURY SPRATS

Serves 4
450 g / 1 lb sprats
salt and freshly ground black pepper
¾ cup / 100 g / 4 oz cream cheese
1 tsp fresh parsley, chopped
1 clove of garlic
1 egg, beaten with 1 tbsp water
dried breadcrumbs
oil for frying

1 Remove the heads from the sprats and open down the belly slit and remove the backbone. Wash the fish under cold running water and drain on kitchen paper towels. Season with salt and pepper.

2 Mix the cream cheese with a little seasoning, chopped parsley and a crushed clove of garlic. Cream the ingredients together well.

3 Stuff the inside of the sprat with a little of the cream cheese mixture and shape the fish by folding over.

4 Dip the fish in beaten egg and then in the crumbs, coating well.

5 Deep fry for about 3 – 4 minutes until golden brown. Drain on absorbent paper.

6 Serve as a party savoury or first course.

Freshwater Fish

Trout with almonds

Salmon (and salmon trout) spend part of their lives in the sea. Cooking methods for these are often interchangeable with those for trout and other river fish. Eel can be fried or grilled (broiled) and served with tartare or béarnaise sauce, and small pike and carp may be cooked 'au bleu'.

Serves 8–10
4 kg / 7–8 lb salmon
½ lemon
½ onion
1 bay leaf
1 sprig parsley
Court-Bouillon (see p 19)

1 Prepare the salmon by slitting the stomach and removing the insides from head to tail. Wash the cavity under cold running water.

Place half a lemon, 2 small pieces of onion, a bay leaf and sprig of parsley in the cavity. (The fish can be gutted by removing the head and drawing the entrails out with the curved handle of a soup ladle. This means the stomach remains whole and is better to dress for a buffet table. However many fish are bought already gutted.)

2 Half fill a fish kettle with the court-bouillon and lower the fish into the cold liquid, bring to the boil gently and then simmer over a low heat for about 45 minutes. Remove from the heat and allow to cool for some hours in the fish liquid.

Do not cook over a high heat or the fish will split.

3 Remove fish from the liquid and allow to drain for about 1 hour if using cold, as a dressed salmon. Alternatively serve the salmon hot with Hollandaise or Mousseline Sauce (see p 21).

ALTERNATIVE METHOD

As fish kettles are fairly large, the smallest being around 40 cm / 18 in, many people do not want the expense of buying one or the storage problem for an occasional large fish. It is possible to cook a fairly large fish in a modern oven if you have a large roasting tin (pan). Pour the court-bouillon to about a quarter of the way up the tin and place the fish diagonally across. The head may be cut off and the tail wrapped in foil to make the fish fit. Cook the head beside the fish. Pour over as much liquid as the tin will take and cover with a double sheet of foil or another large roasting tin.

Allow 10 minutes for each 450 g / 1 lb using this method at *170°C/325°F/Gas 3* . Cool as instructed above.

This method is also used for salmon, trout and sea bass.

TO DRESS A SALMON

1 poached salmon with head and tail
To garnish
2½ cups / 300 ml / ½ pt aspic jelly
1 cucumber
12 stuffed olives
2 lemons
watercress

1 Remove the top skin of the salmon and any grey bits on the pink flesh with the back of a knife.

2 Arrange on a serving platter. Make up the aspic jelly as directed on the packet with boiling water and allow to cool.

3 Paint the salmon over with the aspic and allow to set slightly. After about 30 minutes pour a little more aspic all over the fish. Allow to set.

4 Slice the cucumber very thinly and cut slices in half. Cut the olives into thin slices. The lemon can be marked on the outside with a sharp knife in lines and sliced thinly.

5 Arrange the cucumber slices in a wavy pattern along the edge of the fish. Use the olives to mark the backbone. Paint each slice with aspic before arranging.

Use the halved lemon slices for the other side of the fish, then pour over another coating of almost setting aspic. Any excess aspic may be chopped on the plate around the fish when it has set.

These are only suggestions, and the fish can also be decorated with radishes, hard-boiled (hard-cooked) egg, parsley, halved lemons.

6 Serve the salmon with Mayonnaise or Green Sauce (see pp 22, 23).

SALMON EN CROUTE

Serves 4
1¼ kg / 3 lb tail end of salmon
2½ cups / 600 ml / 1 pt Court-Bouillon (see p 19)
duxelles stuffing
1 medium onion, peeled and finely chopped
6 spring (green) onions, washed and chopped
4 cups / 100 g / 4 oz mushrooms, washed and finely chopped
2 tbsp / 25 g / 1 oz butter
2 tbsp tomato purée (paste)
2 tbsp fish liquor
1 tbsp fresh parsley, chopped
salt and freshly ground pepper
450 g / 1 lb purchased puff pastry, thawed if frozen
Oven temperature 210°C / 425°F / Gas 7.

1 Poach the salmon in the court-bouillon for about 15–20 minutes. Allow to cool in the liquid.

2 Remove the fish and then reduce the liquid by boiling. Skin each side and carefully remove the two top fillets of fish, then lift out the bones and two further fillets will appear underneath. The vegetables for the duxelles stuffing may be chopped in the blender or food processor.

3 Melt the butter in a frying pan and cook the onions and spring onions over a low heat for about 5 minutes. Add the finely chopped mushrooms and continue cooking for a further 3 minutes. Lastly, add the tomato purée and reduced fish liquid, season well and add parsley. Allow to cool.

4 Divide the pastry in two with one piece bigger than the other and roll out the smaller piece. Cut it into a simple fish shape with a slightly pointed nose coming out to a flat head, a rounded body and a fan tail. Make a paper pattern about 30 cm / 12 in long as a guideline, if necessary.

5 Arrange two pieces of fish on the pastry with the broad ends meeting in the middle and the narrower parts at either end. Cover with the duxelles stuffing and then place the other two pieces of fish neatly on top.

6 Roll out the larger half of the pastry about 5 cm / 2 in bigger than the previous piece. Dampen the edges with cold water and place over the fish, tucking the extra pastry underneath and moulding it to secure and improve the fish shape.

7 Cut the remaining strips of pastry into crescents for decoration and thin stips to decorate the tail with fins. Make several slits down the back to allow the steam to escape.

8 Paint with beaten egg, arrange the decorations also glazed with egg, and bake in a hot oven for 20 minutes. If the pastry is browning too quickly, turn down the heat after 15 minutes. Serve with Hollandaise Sauce (see p 21).

SALMON CUTLETS WITH ANCHOVY BUTTER

Serves 4
4 salmon cutlets
4 tbsp / 50 g / 2 oz Anchovy Butter (see p 31)
To garnish
parsley sprigs
4 lemon wedges

1 Pre-heat the grill (broiler) on a high heat.

2 Oil the grill rack and place each steak to ensure an even heat.

3 Place a small knob of Anchovy Butter (divide a quarter of the mixture in four) on each cutlet. Grill (broil) for 4 minutes.

4 Turn the cutlets with a fish slice and place another quarter of the butter among the steaks. Grill on the second side for 4 minutes.

5 Reduce the heat and allow to cook for a further 3 minutes, less if the steaks are thin.

6 Serve with a neatly arranged pat of anchovy butter on top of each cutlet. Garnish with parsley sprigs and lemon wedges.

SALMON FISH CAKES

Makes 12 fish cakes

6 cups / 1 kg / 2 lb peeled and sliced potatoes

250 g / 8 oz cooked salmon, flaked and boned

100 g / 4 oz coley or haddock, cooked, flaked and boned

1 tbsp tomato ketchup

1 tsp Worcestershire sauce

salt and freshly ground pepper

1 tbsp finely chopped parsley

1 egg

Coating

1 egg

2 tbsp water

¾ cup / 75 g / 3 oz dried breadcrumbs

Frying temperature 190°C / 375°F

1 Boil the potatoes until soft, drain and mash through a ricer, a large vegetable mouli or a sieve. It is important that the potato is free from lumps.

2 Mix the flaked fish into the potatoes and gradually add seasonings and the parsley.

3 Finally bind with beaten egg.

4 Flour a board and, using a 5-cm / 2-in scone or cookie cutter, shape the cakes onto a tray or baking sheet. Chill in the freezer or top of the fridge for at least 30 minutes.

5 Flour the hands and dip each cake into the beaten egg mixed with the water, and then coat with the breadcrumbs. Pat the crumbs well into the cakes. Chill for a further 30 minutes.

6 Fry in deep fat for about 4–5 minutes until crisp. Serve with wedges of lemon.

The fried cakes can be refrigerated or frozen and used as required.

Serves 4
4 trout, cleaned
4 tbsp / 150 ml / ¼ pt milk
2 tbsp seasoned flour
4 tbsp / 50 g / 2 oz butter
6 tsp / 100 g / 4 oz flaked almonds
To garnish
4 sprigs parsley
4 sprigs watercress

1 Dip the trout in seasoned milk and then into the flour.

2 Melt 2 tbsp / 25 g / 1 oz butter in a frying pan and lightly fry the almonds — alternatively this can be done without butter in a non-stick frying pan. Shake and turn the almonds to brown evenly. Remove and keep warm.

3 Melt the remaining butter and shallow fry the trout on both sides for about 4 minutes each side. Arrange the almonds on top of the trout during the last 2 minutes of cooking.

Alternatively, remove the top skin showing the pink flesh after cooking and arrange the almonds on top and re-heat for a few minutes under the grill (broiler).

4 Replace fish eye with a sprig of parsley or watercress.

SALMON MOUSSE

Serves 6
250–350 g / 8–12 oz fresh salmon
2½ cups / 600 ml / 1 pt Court-Bouillon (see p 19)
1¼ cups / 300 ml / ½ pt Béchamel Sauce (see p 18)
1¼ cups / 300 ml / ½ pt Mayonnaise (see p 22)
3 tsp gelatine
3 tbsp boiling water
2–3 drops tabasco sauce
1 tbsp tomato ketchup
salt and white pepper
3–4 tbsp double or whipping cream
¼ – ½ cup / 50 g / 2 oz prawns or shrimps (optional)
2 egg whites
150 ml / ¼ pt aspic jelly
To garnish
lettuce / watercress / cucumber / radish / red pimiento, canned

1 Poach the salmon in the court-bouillon. Cool in the liquid, skin and remove bones. Flake the fish and set aside.

2 Make up the béchamel sauce, using half fish liquor and half milk. Make a well seasoned mayonnaise.

3 Dissolve the gelatine by sprinkling onto the hot liquid (never pour the liquid onto the gelatine). Make sure it is completely dissolved.

4 Mix the béchamel sauce and flaked fish together. Add half the mayonnaise and mix well.

5 Add the tabasco sauce and tomato ketchup and season to taste. Add the warm gelatine, the lightly whipped cream and chopped prawns or shrimps.

6 Whisk the egg whites until light and fluffy, but do not overbeat or the mixture will not fold into the mousse. Carefully, with a metal spoon, fold the egg whites into the fish mixture. Turn into an oiled fish mould or ring mould and allow to set in the refrigerator.

7 Turn out onto a serving plate. Mix the remaining mayonnaise with the aspic jelly ; a teaspoon of tomato purée (paste) may be added if liked.

8 Coat the mousse with the mayonnaise mixture and allow to set. Decorate as liked with some lettuce leaves, watercress, thinly sliced cucumber, etc.

Excellent for a cold buffet or starter as well as a delicious summer supper.

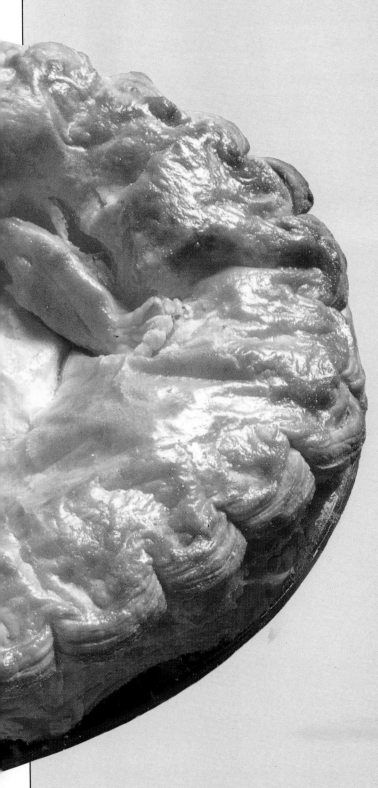

Serves 4
1½ cups / 450 g / 1 lb frozen chopped spinach, cooked
350 g / 12 oz salmon, poached
2½ cups / 600 ml / 1 pt Béchamel Sauce (see p 18)
2 hard-boiled (hard-cooked) eggs
1 tsp dill
1 tbsp chopped parsley
salt and freshly ground black pepper
225 g / 8 oz purchased puff pastry, thawed if frozen
½ beaten egg for glazing
Oven temperature 220°C / 425°F / Gas 7

1 Cook the frozen spinach in a little salted water as directed on the packet. If using fresh spinach you will need to cook approximately 1 kg / 2 lb.

Drain well and line the bottom of a buttered pie plate.

2 Mix the cooked, boned and skinned salmon with the béchamel sauce (which can be made with fish liquor) and chopped hard-boiled eggs. Mix in the dill and parsley and pour the mixture on top of the spinach.

3 Roll out the puff pastry 5 cm / 2 in larger than the pie plate. Cut a 2½-cm / 1-in wide strip from the outer edge of the pastry. Brush the rim of the plate with water and fit the pastry strip around. Lift the remaining piece of pastry over the rolling pin and transfer to the pie plate. Press the edges together and trim with a sharp knife held at an angle away from the dish. To seal the edges firmly together hold the knife horizontally towards the pie plate and make a series of shallow cuts round the edge. Flute the edges with the thumb and forefinger and pull in the flutes with the back of a knife.

4 To make decorative leaves for a savoury pastry pie, cut remaining pastry into 3½-cm / 1½-in strips using the rolling pin or ruler as a guide. Every 5 cm / 2½ in cut the strips at an angle to make diamond shapes. Press lines on the diamonds to make the veins of the leaves.

5 Make a hole in the middle of the pie by making a cross with a knife and fold back each part, arrange the leaves in a decorative pattern around the middle and brush with beaten egg.

6 Bake in a pre-heated oven until pastry is well risen and golden brown — approximately 30 minutes. Cover with foil or waxed greaseproof paper if pastry shows any sign of browning too much.

Serves 4
450 g / 1 lb salmon or salmon trout
4 tbsp / 50 g / 2 oz butter
salt and freshly ground pepper
8 spring (green) onions, washed and chopped or 1 onion, finely chopped
⅔ cup / 100 g / 4 oz cooked rice
2 cups / 100 g / 4 oz mushrooms, washed and sliced
2 hard-boiled (hard-cooked) eggs
grated rind and juice of ½ lemon
1 tbsp fresh dill or 1 tsp dried
1 tbsp chopped parsley
2 tbsp sour cream
450 g / 1 lb purchased puff pastry, thawed if frozen
1 egg, beaten
Oven temperature 150°C / 300°F / Gas 2 for salmon; 220°C / 450°F / Gas 8 for pastry for 10 minutes, reducing to 200°C / 400°F / Gas 6

1 Cut half the butter into small pieces and dab over salmon, season and wrap loosely in foil. Place in a pre-heated oven for 25–30 minutes. Unwrap and allow to cool.

2 Melt the remaining butter and add the spring onions or very finely chopped onion. Gradually stir in the cooked rice and mushrooms. Allow to cool.

3 Remove skin and bones carefully from salmon and leave in large flakes.

4 Mix the salmon in a bowl with the cooked rice and mushrooms, chopped hard-boiled egg, grated rind and juice of ½ lemon, dill, parsley and seasoning. Lastly add the sour cream.

5 Roll the pastry into two halves 35 cm × 35 cm / 14 in × 14 in. Cut into 17½-cm / 7-in squares. Place the mixture in the middle of each square and turn dampened corners over and crimp the edges. Brush with beaten egg and place on a baking sheet in a hot oven for about 20 minutes.

6 Serve garnished with watercress and baked mushrooms, and accompanied by Hollandaise Sauce (see p 21) or a jug of sour cream mixed with fresh chives.

TROUT CHAUDFROID

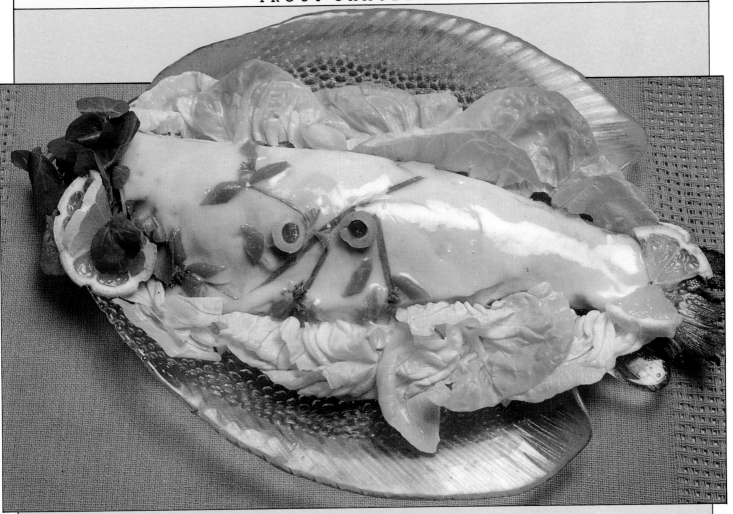

Serves 4
4 trout
1 ¼ cups / 300 ml / ½ pt chaudfroid sauce
To garnish
cucumber peel
canned pimiento
stuffed olives, sliced
watercress

1 Cook the trout 'au bleu' (see p 70) and allow to cool.

2 Remove the heads and top skin. Lift top fillet from fish carefully and remove the bone. Lay fillet back on the fish.

3 Coat with sauce. Garnish with cucumber peel cut into thin strips, diamond-shaped pieces of pimiento, and sliced stuffed olives to make flowers and leaves. Surround head end with sprigs of watercress. An excellent summer meal or buffet dish.

Serves 4
650 g / 1½ lb pike or grey mullet
4 eggs
1 cup / 4 oz flour
1¼ cups / 300 ml / ½ pt milk
4 tbsp / 50 g / 2 oz butter
4 tbsp / 50 g / 2 oz suet
salt and freshly ground pepper
3 tbsp double or whipping cream

Quenelles are traditionally made with pike but other fish can be used. It is a rather difficult dish to make by hand and is easier if a food processor is used.

1 Remove skin and bones from the fish.

2 Make a thick mixture by stirring 2 eggs, sieved flour and milk together. Beat briskly over a low heat, add butter and stir until a thick mixture is made, almost like a choux pastry. Allow to cool.

3 Place the fish in the food processor and pulverize.

4 Add the suet, then the flour mixture.

5 Season, then add the 2 egg yolks and mix well in the processor. Add lightly beaten cream.

6 Wet a board and make the mixture into small sausage-sized portions. If the mixture is not holding together add a whisked egg white.

7 Bring a saucepan of salted water to the boil and reduce to simmering. Drop the quenelles into the water. Cook for a few minutes (never boil) and test one for taste.

8 Serve with 2½ cups / 600 ml / 1 pt Béchamel Sauce (see p 18) with 1 tbsp tomato purée (paste) added with 100 g / 4 oz prawns or shrimps.

STEAMED TROUT WITH HAZELNUTS AND COURGETTES (ZUCCHINI)

Serves 2
2 × 450-g / 1-lb trout
2 courgettes (zucchini)
juice of ½ lemon
bunch of fresh chives
½ cup / 100 ml / 4 fl oz hazelnut oil
scant ¼ cup / 25 g / 1 oz hazelnuts

1 Fillet the trout or ask the fish shop to do this. Place the fillets which have no skin or bones left on a plate or dish which will fit over a saucepan to steam (see p 14) skinned side down.

2 Cut the courgettes into matchstick pieces and sprinkle with a little of the lemon juice. Place the courgettes on top of the fish. Steam the fish for about 8 minutes or until cooked.

3 Meanwhile, snip the chives into small pieces, mix with the remaining lemon juice, hazelnut oil and the hazelnuts which have been put into a blender. Alternatively, place the nuts in the blender or food processor and blend, then add the other ingredients to mix well.

4 Remove trout onto warmed plates and sprinkle with the hazelnut dressing.

Serve with boiled new potatoes and a crisp green salad.

Freshwater Fish

TROUT 'AU BLEU'

Serves 4
4⅜ cups / 1 l / 1¾ pt Court-Bouillon (see p 21)
⅝ cup / 150 ml / ¼ pt white wine vinegar

1 Gut the trout just before cooking but do not scale. Place in a saucepan.

2 Pour on white wine vinegar, add lukewarm, well-seasoned Court-Bouillon and allow to simmer for about 10 minutes. Do not allow to boil or the fish will split. Serve with lemon wedges and Hollandaise Sauce (see p 21).

Seafish

There are many varieties of seafish available all the year round as much of the catch is frozen at sea. This means that areas which are not well served for fresh fish are still able to offer a good selection of frozen in the supermarkets and freezer stores.
Recipes using flat fish such as different types of sole can be varied as can the larger white fish which may be sold in fillets, steaks or cutlets.

SOLE EN GOUJON

Serves 4 or 8 as a cocktail savoury
4 sole, filleted and skinned
flour or matzo flour to coat
egg, beaten
1 tbsp water
dried breadcrumbs
oil for frying
Frying temperature 190°C/375°F

1 Cut the fish fillet into two pieces and then cut each half in strips diagonally.

2 Flour the strips and shake off excess. Then dip in egg before rolling in the breadcrumbs.

3 Deep fry until golden brown.

4 Serve as a cocktail savoury or as a fish appetizer with lemon wedges.

Can be accompanied with Seafood Sauce or Tartare Sauce (see pp 23, 24).

Sole en goujon

WHITING BERCY

Serves 4
4 × 300-g / 10-oz whiting
4 tbsp / 50 g / 2 oz butter
2 small onions
⅝ cup / 150 ml / ¼ pt white wine
1 tbsp fresh parsley, chopped
juice of ½ lemon
salt and freshly ground pepper
1 tbsp / 150 g / ½ oz butter
½ cup / 15 g / ½ oz flour
½ cup / 25 g / 1 oz fresh breadcrumbs
To garnish
lemon slices

1 Fillet the fish and make the fish stock with the trimmings and heads (see p 18).

2 Fold fillets over with a small knob of butter in each and poach in the fish stock for about 8 minutes. Remove fillets and keep warm.

3 Melt the remaining butter and toss in finely chopped onion for a few minutes; cook on a low heat without browning. Add the wine and allow to reduce slightly. Finally add the strained fish stock, chopped parsley, juice of ½ lemon, salt and pepper.

Bring to the boil and remove from the heat. Knead together the butter and flour and whisk into the liquid.

Whisk on the heat for a few minutes until sauce thickens. Pour over fillets which have been kept warm.

4 Sprinkle with breadcrumbs and top with little knobs of butter.

Place in a hot oven or brown under the grill (broiler) for a few minutes.

May be made with sole or cod.

FILLETS OF SOLE IN WHITE WINE WITH MUSHROOMS

Serves 4
4 lemon sole, filleted
⅝ cup / 150 ml / ¼ pt white wine
⅝ cup / 150 ml / ¼ pt water
1 small onion, peeled and sliced
6 small mushrooms
1 bay leaf
sprig of parsley
4 peppercorns
1 tbsp / 15 g / ½ oz butter
2 tbsp / 15 g / ½ oz flour
2 tbsp single (cereal) cream
Oven temperature 170°C / 350°F / Gas 4

1 Roll the fillets of sole head to tail and arrange in an ovenproof dish.

2 Pour over the wine, water, onion, mushroom stalks, herbs and seasoning. Cook in a moderate oven covered with a buttered paper or foil or lid for 15–20 minutes.

3 Strain the liquid from the fish and make up to 1¼ cups / 300 ml / ½ pt with water or wine if necessary. Poach the mushroom caps in this liquid for a few minutes — remove and keep warm.

4 Make a roux with the butter and flour and make up a sauce with the fish liquid.

5 Add the cream to the sauce just before serving, pour over the warmed fish, and serve with Duchesse potatoes, mushroom caps and sprigs of watercress.

Serves 4

2 lemon or Dover soles, filleted
½ cup / 50 g / 2 oz flour
4 tbsp / 50 g / 2 oz butter
1 tbsp fresh parsley, chopped
1 lemon

1 Flour the fillets of sole and shake off excess.

2 Melt the butter and shallow fry the fillets for about 3 minutes either side.

3 Arrange the fillets on a warm serving dish and keep warm.

4 Add the parsley to the butter in the pan. Add a little extra butter if necessary.

Pour over the fish and serve with wedges of lemon.

Serves 4

4 tbsp / 50 g / 2 oz butter
1 onion, peeled and chopped
3 tomatoes, peeled and chopped
8 fillets of sole
salt and freshly ground pepper
⅝ cup / 150 ml / ¼ pt white wine
2 tbsp / 15 g / ½ oz flour

To garnish

1 tomato, peeled and sliced
few sprigs of parsley

1 Melt 2 tbsp / 25 g / 1 oz butter in a frying pan and add the chopped onions. Sweat over a low heat for a few minutes. Add the tomatoes and simmer for a further 2 minutes.

2 Fold the fish in three and lay on top of the tomato and onion mixture, add seasoning and white wine and simmer for a further 12 minutes.

3 Remove the fish to a serving dish and keep warm. Reduce the sauce by about half over a medium heat.

4 Make a roux with the remaining butter and flour. Add the sieved liquid to make a sauce. Arrange the sole on a plate with Duchesse potatoes and mask with the sauce.

Garnish with sliced tomatoes and sprigs of parsley.

Seafish

FAMILY FISH PIE

Serves 4
450 g / 1 lb haddock or cod, filleted
1¼ cups / 300 ml / ½ pt milk or milk and water for Béchamel Sauce (see p 18)
2 tomatoes, skinned and sliced
1 cup / 50 g / 2 oz mushrooms, washed and sliced
salt and freshly ground pepper
6 cups / 1 kg / 2 lb potatoes, peeled and sliced
1 egg
2 tbsp milk
2 tbsp / 25 g / 1 oz butter or margarine
To garnish
parsley sprigs
Oven temperature 180°C / 350°F / Gas 4

1 Poach the fish in the milk or milk and water. Allow to cool in the liquid. Strain the liquid into a measuring jug and make up to 1¼ cups / 300 ml / ½ pt if necessary for the béchamel sauce.

2 Remove the skin from the fish, and flake.

3 Arrange the tomatoes and mushrooms on the bottom of a pie plate. Make up the sauce, season well, mix with the fish and pour into the pie plate.

4 Cook, mash and sieve or mouli the potatoes, mix with a little beaten egg and milk, season well. Pipe or pile on top of the fish mixture and dot with the butter or margarine. Bake in moderate oven for about 25 minutes.

Seafish

FAMILY FISH PIE

VARIATION

For a more elaborate dinner party fish pie, a variety of fish may be used and the topping can either be the potato mixture or 250 g / 8 oz purchased puff pastry.

Use 450 g / 1 lb white fish — haddock, cod, sole, turbot — and cook it in a mixture of wine and water to make a richer sauce. Add ¼ cup / 50 g / 2 oz smoked salmon pieces and ¾ cup / 100 g / 4 oz prawns or shrimps to the sauce which may be flavoured with 2 tsp tomato purée (paste).

SOLE VERONIQUE

Serves 4
Stuffing
¾ – 1 cup / 100 g / 4 oz green grapes
2 tbsp / 25 g / 1 oz butter
½ small onion, diced
2 tbsp breadcrumbs
salt and freshly ground pepper
1 kg / 2 lb whole sole
1 bay leaf
1 small onion, peeled and sliced
6 peppercorns
salt
⅝ cup / 150 ml / ¼ pt white wine or white wine and water
1¼ cups / 300 ml / ½ pt Velouté Sauce (see p 18) made from fish liquor and milk
2 tbsp single (cereal) cream
To garnish
green grapes
watercress
Oven temperature 180°C / 350°F / Gas 4

1 Dip the grapes in boiling water for about 5 seconds. Cut in half, remove skin and discard the seeds.

2 To make the stuffing, melt the butter and sweat the onion over a low heat for about 4 minutes. Mix with breadcrumbs and about ½ cup / 50 g / 2 oz chopped green grapes and seasoning.

3 Fillet the fish and wrap them skinned side inwards around stuffing. Lay in an ovenproof dish and add bay leaf, onion and seasonings; finally, pour on the wine.
   Add enough fish stock to come half way up the dish.

4 When the fish is cooked, remove the fillets and keep warm. Place the liquid in a saucepan and reduce to about ⅝ cup / 150 ml / ¼ pt. Make 300 ml / ½ pt of velouté sauce from the fish liquor and milk.

5 Finally add the cream to the slightly cooled sauce and pour over the fish.

Decorate with green grapes and sprigs of watercress. If sole is unavailable use plaice.

SKATE IN CAPER SAUCE

Serves 4
4 wings of skate
1¼ cups / 300 ml / ½ pt water
1 tbsp vinegar
1 small onion, peeled and sliced
1 bay leaf
salt and freshly ground pepper
1 tbsp / 15 g / ½ oz butter
2 tbsp / 15 g / ½ oz flour
3 tbsp capers, chopped
2 tbsp fresh parsley, chopped
Oven temperature 180°C / 350°F / Gas 4

1 Place the skate wings in a baking dish and pour over the water, vinegar, sliced onion and bay leaf. Season with salt and pepper.

2 Cook covered in the oven for about 15–20 minutes.

3 In a saucepan make a roux with the butter and flour to make up a sauce with 1¼ cups / 300 ml / ½ pt of the fish liquor, strained from the skate. Add the chopped capers and parsley.

Pour the sauce over the fish and serve with sauté potatoes and a crisp green vegetable.

If skate is unavailable use halibut or turbot.

RED MULLET PROVENCAL

Serves 2
4 red mullet
2 tbsp / 25 g / 1 oz butter
1¼ cups / 300 ml / ½ pt Tomato Sauce (see p 28)
1 green or red pepper, deseeded and diced
1 tbsp port or sherry
salt and freshly ground pepper
stoned black olives
To garnish
lemon wedges
4 anchovy fillets
Oven temperature 180°C / 350°F / Gas 4

1 Rub the fish with melted butter and place under a hot grill (broiler) for 2 minutes each side.

2 Arrange in an ovenproof dish.

3 Mix the tomato sauce with the diced pepper and the port. Season the fish well and pour over the sauce, then arrange the olives.

4 Bake for 20 minutes. Serve hot, garnished with lemon wedges and anchovy fillets, or serve chilled as an hors d'oeuvre.

Red mullet or rouget as it is known in France has a very delicate taste and is best prepared simply either by grilling (broiling) or baking in foil. It has no gall and does not need to be cleaned; indeed the liver is considered a delicacy.

ROAST GREY MULLET

Serves 4
1 kg / 2 lb grey mullet, gutted and cleaned
4 tbsp / 50 g / 2 oz Green Butter (see p 30)
½ lemon, sliced
1 small onion, peeled and quartered
fresh thyme sprigs
sprigs of parsley
Oven temperature 180°C / 350°F / Gas 4

1 Butter the fish inside and out with the Green butter.

2 Arrange lemon slices, quartered onion, sprig of thyme and the parsley in the stomach slit.

3 Make an S-shaped cut in the fish back and stuff the thyme sprigs into it.

4 Bake for 25 minutes. Serve with Gribiche Sauce and Green Butter (see pp 22, 30)

The fish may be cooked wrapped in foil, if preferred.

RED SNAPPER A LA CREOLE

Serves 4
1½ kg / 2–3 lb red snapper
salt and freshly ground pepper
juice of 1 lemon
few sprigs of thyme
bayleaf
sprig parsley
4 allspice berries, crushed
4 cloves
Stuffing
½ onion
2 tbsp / 25 g / 1 oz butter
mushroom stalks from the 2½ cups / 100 g / 4 oz mushrooms, chopped
2 tbsp breadcrumbs
1 tbsp chopped parsley
salt and freshly ground pepper
Sauce
⅝ cup / 150 ml / ¼ pt white wine
2 tbsp / 25 g / 1 oz butter
1 large onion, peeled and finely chopped
2 large fresh tomatoes, peeled
2½ cups / 100 g / 4 oz mushrooms, sliced
1½ cups / 425-g / 15-oz can of tomatoes
To garnish
chopped parsley
Oven temperature 170°C / 350°F / Gas 4

1 Clean and wash the snapper thoroughly. Sprinkle inside and out with seasoning and lemon juice.
   Make an S-shaped cut in the back and stuff with thyme, bay leaf, parsley, allspice and cloves.

2 Make the stuffing by sweating the onion in the butter until it is translucent, about 4 minutes on a low heat. Add chopped mushroom stalks and continue cooking for a further 2 minutes.

3 Add the breadcrumbs, parsley and seasoning. Put the stuffing into the fish stomach.

4 Lay the fish in a flat dish and pour over the wine. Bake for about 20 minutes covered with a lid or a piece of foil.

5 Meanwhile melt the butter in a frying pan, add the chopped onion and cook until it is transparent. Add the chopped fresh tomatoes and sliced mushrooms and cook for a few minutes on a low heat. Then add the canned tomatoes, season and simmer for about 10 minutes.

6 After the fish has cooked for 20 minutes pour over the sauce and continue cooking for a further 10–15 minutes.

Serve sprinkled with chopped parsley.

The classic creole recipe for this dish has oysters and shrimps added to the sauce at stage 5.

FISH KEBABS ON RICE WITH SPICY TOMATO SAUCE

Serves 4

2 thick cod steaks

8 medium mushrooms

8 bay leaves

8 cooked prawns or shrimps

1 green pepper, deseeded

1 red or yellow pepper, deseeded

2 courgettes (zucchini), thickly sliced

Marinade

4 tbsp oil

6 tbsp lemon juice

salt and freshly ground pepper

1 tbsp roughly chopped parsley

1 bay leaf

1 small onion, thinly sliced in rings

½ tsp paprika

1¼ cups / 25 g / 8 oz long grain rice, uncooked

½ tsp turmeric

To garnish

lemon wedges

parsley sprigs

1 Cut the cod steaks into 12 even-sized pieces and thread onto the skewers one piece at a time. Alternate with mushrooms, bay leaves, prawns or shrimps, squares of blanched pepper and slices of courgette.

2 Make up the marinade and pour over the fish. Leave to marinate for at least 3 hours and turn the kebabs from time to time.

3 Add 4 cups of water with turmeric added to the rice and cook as directed on the packet or see Paella (see p 24).

4 Paint the grill (broiler) rack with oil to prevent food sticking and grill (broil) the skewered food for about 4 minutes each side until the cod is cooked. Serve on a warm bed of rice with Spicy Tomato Sauce (see p 27) and a crisp green salad.

SALAD NICOISE

Serves 4

2 large / 450 g / 1 lb potatoes, boiled

2 cups / 250 g / 8 oz green beans, fresh or frozen

1 × 200-g / 7-oz can tuna fish

⅝ cup / 150 ml / ¼ pt vinaigrette

4 tomatoes, skinned and sliced

¼ cucumber

2 hard-boiled (hard-cooked) eggs

12 black or green olives, stones removed

6 anchovy fillets, cut into thin slices

To garnish

small cherry tomatoes

1 Cook the potatoes in their skins until tender. Remove the skins and dice finely. Cook the beans in a small amount of boiling water for about 6 minutes. Frozen beans can be used; cook as directed on the packet.

2 Mix the potatoes, beans and half the tuna fish with three-quarters of the vinaigrette.

3 Arrange the sliced tomatoes on the bottom and around the bowl, arrange thinly sliced cucumber on top, and sprinkle with a little vinaigrette. Place a few chunks of tuna fish on the tomato and cucumber.

4 The eggs may be cut into slices or wedges and can be used on top as a garnish or arranged to make a bed for the beans, potatoes and tuna fish mixture.

5 Arrange the fish mixture in the middle and arrange the anchovies in a diamond-shaped pattern on the beans, decorating each space with an olive. Pour over any remaining dressing.

This makes a delicious lunch, appetizer for dinner party or buffet salad, with crispy French bread.

Makes 16 croquettes
500 g / 1 lb smoked haddock or cod
⅝ cup / 150 ml / ¼ pt milk
1 small onion, finely chopped, or 6 spring (green) onions
4½ cups / 675 g / 1½ lb potatoes, peeled and cooked
1 hard-boiled (hard-cooked) egg
few drops Worcester sauce
1 tbsp parsley, chopped
1 egg, beaten
1½ cups / 125 g / 4 oz dried breadcrumbs
oil for frying

1 Poach the smoked haddock or cod in a little milk and a knob of butter. Allow the fish to cool in the liquid then remove and flake the fish into a bowl.

2 If using an onion in place of spring onions sweat in butter until cooked but do not allow to brown. Alternatively chop up the spring onions and add to the fish mixture raw.

3 Sieve or put the potatoes through a mouli or ricer to prevent lumps, and add 4 tbsp of fish liquid. Add the chopped hard-boiled egg, Worcester sauce, chopped parsley, a shake of pepper. Taste before salting as the fish may be salty.

Mix the ingredients well.

With floured hands form into sausage-shape rounds about 5 cm / 2 in long. Chill in the fridge and then coat in egg and crumbs.

4 Fry in hot oil and serve with crisp vegetables or a salad.

It is useful to make up double batches and store in the freezer until needed.

Serves 4
50 g / 1 lb smoked haddock
1¼ cups / 300 ml / ½ pt milk
2 tbsp / 25 g / 1 oz butter
4 tbsp / 25 g / 1 oz flour
salt and freshly ground pepper
pinch of cayenne pepper
pinch of grated nutmeg
4 egg yolks
2 tbsp single (cereal) cream
6 egg whites
Oven temperature 190°C / 375°F / Gas 5

1 Poach the smoked haddock in the milk with a quarter of the butter for about 10 minutes over a low heat (see p 14) until cooked.

2 Drain the liquid and make up to 1¼ cups / 300 ml / ½ pt with a little water if necessary. Skin and flake the fish.

3 Melt the remaining butter in a saucepan and make a roux with the flour. Season the fish liquid and add the cayenne and nutmeg. Be careful with the salt as smoked fish can be salty. Add the fish liquor to the roux and make a thick smooth sauce. Add a little of the warm sauce to the egg yolks mixed with the cream and then return to the sauce. Lastly add the flaked fish.

4 Prepare a 17-cm / 7-in soufflé dish by oiling well — place the other half of the fish in the bottom of the dish. Whisk the egg whites until fluffy but not too stiff and fold carefully into the mixture. Turn into the soufflé dish and cook for about 30 – 35 minutes.

Serve immediately with a crisp salad for lunch or supper, or as the fish course or appetizer for a dinner party.

Seafish

TUNA–STUFFED POTATOES

Serves 4
4 large potatoes, scrubbed
4 tomatoes, skinned and chopped
4 spring (green) onions, washed and chopped
4 tbsp sour cream
salt and freshly ground pepper
scant cup / 1 × 200-g / 7-oz can tuna fish, in oil
Oven temperature 180°C / 350°F / Gas 4

1 Make a cross on the potato skins and bake for 1 hour or until cooked.

2 Halve the potatoes and scoop out the cooked potato, retaining the skins.

3 Mix all ingredients together, season well and arrange in the potato skins.

4 Re-heat before serving.

Tuna-stuffed potatoes

STUFFED BAKED MACKEREL

Serves 4
4 mackerel
salt and freshly ground pepper
2 tbsp lemon juice
4 tbsp oil
1 medium onion
¾ – 1 cup / 100 g / 4 oz gooseberries, fresh or canned
4 level tbsp breadcrumbs
1 tbsp chopped parsley
1 tsp chopped mint
salt and freshly ground pepper
2 tbs / 25 g / 1 oz butter
To garnish
wedges of lemon
Oven temperature 200°C / 400°F / Gas 6 reducing to 180°C / 350°F / Gas 4

1 Clean the fish, remove head, slit down the stomach and remove backbone. Sprinkle with salt, pepper and a little of the lemon juice.

2 Heat 2 tbsp oil and fry finely chopped onions, then add the gooseberries and mix well.

3 Mix breadcrumbs, parsley, mint, lemon juice and seasoning together, add onion and gooseberries and mix well.

4 Stuff into mackerel and secure edges together with a cocktail stick or toothpick.

5 Place fish in remaining oil in a casserole, dot with butter and bake in a hot oven for 15 minutes then reduce heat and cook for a further 15–20 minutes until fish is tender.

SOUSED HERRINGS ('SOLOMON GUNDY')

Serves 4
8 herrings, filleted
1 level tsp salt
freshly ground pepper
1 tsp allspice
8 peppercorns, slightly crushed
1 bay leaf
300 ml / ½ pt vinegar
300 ml / ½ pt water
Oven temperature 170°C / 325°F / Gas 3

1 Fillet the herrings (see p 11) or ask the fish shop to do this for you. Season the inside of the washed herring.

2 Roll the fish from head to tail and secure with a wooden cocktail stick or toothpick. Arrange fish in a baking dish or casserole.

3 Place the remaining ingredients in a saucepan, bring to the boil and simmer for 5 minutes then allow to cool slightly.

4 Pour onto the fish and bake in the oven covered either with foil or a lid for about 1 hour.

Allow to cool in the liquid and serve with a green salad.

HERRINGS IN OATMEAL WITH MUSTARD SAUCE

Serves 4
4 herrings, filleted
4 tbsp milk
1 tbsp seasoned flour
1 egg, beaten
⅔ cup / 50 g / 2 oz coarse oatmeal
Mustard Sauce (see p 29)
oil for frying

1 Fillet the herrings (see p 11) or ask the fish shop to do this for you. Wash thoroughly under cold running water.

2 Steep the herring in the milk for about half an hour, drain and dip in seasoned flour.

3 Dip the fish in beaten egg and then coat generously in coarse oatmeal.

4 Shallow fry in hot oil, stomach side down first, until crisp and golden on either side. Serve with wedges of lemon and mustard sauce. New potatoes are usually served with this dish.

DEVILLED HERRING

Serves 4
4 herrings, filleted
4 tsp French mustard
4 tsp breadcrumbs
Sauce
⅝ cup/150 ml/¼ pt vegetable oil
3 tbsp white wine vinegar
1 tsp capers, chopped
½ tsp tarrragon, dried
1 spring (green) onion, finely chopped
salt and freshly ground pepper

1 Pre-heat the grill (broiler). Make 3 slits in the backs of each of the boned herrings. Arrange on the grill (broiler) pan.

2 Spread the mustard over the fish and sprinkle with breadcrumbs. Brush with a little vegetable oil and grill under a high heat for 5 minutes. Lower heat to medium and continue cooking for a further 5 minutes.

3 Place all the sauce ingredients in a screw-top jar and shake well. Serve separately in a sauceboat either hot or cold.

SARDINES PROVENCAL

Serves 4
1 kg/2 lb fresh or frozen sardines
salt and freshly ground pepper
4 tbsp fresh breadcrumbs
1 tsp anchovy essence
1 tsp mixed fresh herbs or ½ tsp dried
1 tsp freshly chopped parsley
2 eggs, beaten
1 kg/2 lb spinach
2 tsp vegetable oil
2 tbsp single (cereal) cream
2 tbsp Parmesan cheese
2 tsp vegetable oil
Oven temperature 180°C/350°F/Gas 4

1 Allow sardines to thaw (if using frozen). Slit down the stomach and remove the backbone. Season each and leave open.

2 Mix 2 tbsp breadcrumbs, seasoning, anchovy essence and herbs in a bowl and add a little of the beaten egg.

3 Place some of this mixture in each fish and fold over to reshape.

4 Blanch the spinach for 2 minutes if using fresh and for 4 if using frozen in boiling water. Drain carefully.

5 Season well with salt and pepper. Mix with cream and remaining egg. Arrange spinach in the bottom of an ovenproof dish with the sardines on top. Sprinkle the fish with a mixture of 2 tbsp breadcrumbs and 2 tsp Parmesan cheese. Brush with oil and cook in the oven until the fish are golden brown.

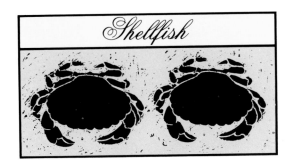

Shellfish

Shellfish are divided in two categories:

Molluscs — shellfish with shells but no limbs, eg scallops, mussels and oysters. Squid are also molluscs.

Crustaceans — shellfish which have a shell but also have limbs, eg crabs, crayfish, lobsters and prawns.

Most shellfish are sold by the fish shop cooked except for oysters, scallops and mussels. Live lobsters can be specially ordered. Shellfish are now available throughout the year although different coastal areas have different seasonal times. It is advisable to order fresh shellfish as many fish shops do not keep large stocks because shellfish deteriorate very quickly. Care must be taken not to overcook shellfish or they become rubbery.

Some parts of shellfish are unsuitable for eating. These are the gills and the grey spongy parts known as 'dead man's fingers' in lobsters and crabs, and the beards attached to scallops and mussels. The fish shop will either clean the shellfish for you or explain how to do so and what to remove if the customer is unsure.

Fresh, frozen and cooked oysters are now available all the year round. Oysters should be opened with a small sharp-pointed knife. Hold the oyster in the palm of the hand, insert the knife at the hinge and twist to open. Open oysters over a bowl to catch the juice.

Fresh scallops are usually sold already opened and with the beard removed. Frozen scallops are available throughout the year.

Mussels should not be used if the shells are damaged or open. They should close when the shell is tapped firmly. Wash thoroughly and remove beards as directed in mussels recipe (see p 110). Discard any mussels which do not open when cooked.

Crabs are available all the year round. To cook a fresh crab, plunge it in fast-boiling salted water. Medium size crabs about 12–15 cm/5–6 in have the best flavour; smaller ones have very little meat and larger ones tend to have rather coarse meat.

OYSTERS

Most people prefer to eat oysters 'au naturel', that is, raw from the shell with a squeeze of lemon. However, there are also many delicious cooked dishes for oyster lovers.

OYSTERS A L'AMERICAINE

Serves 4
24 oysters
2 cups / 100 g / 4 oz fresh breadcrumbs
4 tbsp / 50 g / 2 oz butter
freshly ground black pepper
1 cup / 100 g / 4 oz Gruyère cheese, grated
Oven temperature 220°C / 425°F / Gas 7

1 Remove the oysters from the shell and wash the deep shells thoroughly. Drain and wipe the oysters on kitchen paper towels.

2 Fry half the breadcrumbs in melted butter until golden brown. Sprinkle a few fried breadcrumbs in the bottom of 24 shells. Season with pepper. Return oysters to shells, sprinkle with a mixture of breadcrumbs and Gruyère cheese and brown in a hot oven.

Serve immediately.

OYSTERS EN BROCHETTE

Serves 4
24 oysters
1¼ cups / 300 ml / ½ pt dry white wine and water
1 tbsp oil
12 slices of bacon, de-rinded
freshly ground black pepper
4 slices of toast, cut in long strips
1 cup / 50 g / 2 oz fresh white breadcrumbs
2 tbsp / 25 g / 1 oz butter
¾ tsp cayenne pepper

1 Drain the opened oysters over a sieve lined with muslin to catch the oyster juice. Heat the wine and water and oyster liquid in a saucepan and add a shake of pepper.

2 Allow the oysters to remain in the liquid for a few minutes without boiling. Remove when plumped up.

3 Cut the bacon slices in half and stretch with a knife, and cook in a little oil over a low heat until the fat starts to run. Do not crisp.

4 Wrap the bacon around the oysters and thread onto skewers.

5 Place the skewers under a hot grill (broiler) for a few minutes, turning from time to time.

6 Place on the long strips of toast, and keep warm.

7 Fry the breadcrumbs in the butter until golden and mix with cayenne. Sprinkle on the brochettes and serve immediately.

This recipe can also be made with mussels.

LOBSTER

LOBSTER

To prepare and cook a live lobster. Take a skewer or sharp knife and drive through the cross which is on the head. Grip the lobster firmly behind the head and plunge into a large saucepan of boiling salted water. A bay leaf, sprig of parsley or bouquet garni may be added. Cook for 15 minutes for each 500 g / 1 lb of lobster. Allow to cool in the liquid. Leave the antennae on the lobster as they form part of the decoration if serving in the shell. When cool, twist off the claws, retaining small claws for garnish.

DRESSED LOBSTER

1 Crack the pincer claws with a small hammer and take out the meat with a skewer.

2 Cut the lobster lengthways from head to tail using a sharp knife. Remove the stomach bag on the right side of the head and remove the grey spongy parts known as 'dead man's fingers'.

3 Remove the coral, wash and retain for decoration.

4 Now remove all the meat from the shell. Keep the green liver meat which is edible.

5 Flavour the meat with lemon juice and seasoning or mayonnaise and return to the shell. Serve on a platter of lettuce.

Lobsters are best at about 650 g – 1 kg / 1¾ – 2½ lb as this will give two good servings or about 400 g / ¾ lb meat. A well cooked lobster will feel heavy and the tail should be curled under the body.

   Prawns and shrimps have become a general term for several kinds of shellfish from small shrimps to the larger Dublin Bay prawns. They are usually sold cooked and are widely available frozen.

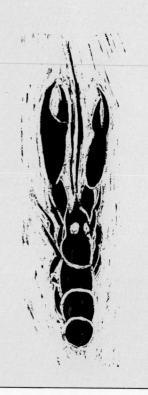

Most hot lobster dishes are best made with freshly cooked lobster which means killing the lobster just before cooking it. For those who find this difficult the delicious Lobster Newburg is a welcome recipe as it can be made with a cooked lobster bought from the fish shop.

Serves 4
1 kg / 2 lb lobster, cooked
2 tbsp / 25 g / 1 oz butter
salt and freshly ground pepper
2 tbsp brandy
3 egg yolks
⅝ cup / 150 ml / ¼ pt double or whipping cream
1½ cups / 275 g / 10 oz cooked rice
To garnish
1 tbsp chopped parsley
lemon twists

1 Cut down the soft shell under the tail with scissors. Peel away the hard shell to leave the tail whole.

2 Crack the claws with a small hammer and carefully remove the meat with a skewer.

3 Melt half the butter in a frying pan over a very low heat. Add the claw meat and the tail meat cut in sections, season well and heat through for about 3 minutes.

4 Heat the brandy in a ladle and set it alight to 'flambé' the lobster by pouring the lighted brandy onto the lobster meat. When the flames die down remove the pan from the heat.

5 Mix egg yolks, cream and the remaining butter cut into little pieces with more seasoning.

6 Return the lobster meat to the lower heat and gradually pour over egg mixture, stirring with wooden spoon until the sauce becomes thick and creamy.

Serve on hot boiled rice garnished with parsley and lemon twist.

Serves 4
approx 1 kg / 4 lb mussels
4 tbsp / 50 g / 2 oz butter
1 medium onion, finely chopped
1–2 cloves of garlic, finely crushed
1¼ cups / 250 ml / ½ pt white wine
1 bay leaf
fresh sprigs parsley
2 tbsp chopped parsley, optional
2 tbsp cream, optional

1 Make sure the mussels are properly prepared before cooking. They should be alive — tap with a wooden spoon and if any remain open discard at once.

Wash and scrub the shells thoroughly under a cold running tap and remove the beard. Place in a bowl of cold water and change the water several times to remove the sand.

2 Heat butter in a very large saucepan or frying pan. Add the chopped onion and garlic. Allow to sweat gently in the butter without browning.

3 Add the wine, bay leaf and sprigs of parsley. Turn up the heat and add the cleaned mussels. Shake over the heat for about 6–10 minutes until all the mussels are open.
Discard any mussels which do not open. Divide the mussels into serving bowls and if liked add the cream and the parsley to the juice. Heat for a further minute and pour over the mussels.

Serve with warm French bread and extra plates for empty shells.

SHELLFISH QUICHE

Serves 4–6
Shortcrust Pastry
1½ cups / 175 g / 6 oz flour
4 tbsp / 50 g / 2 oz butter or hard margarine
3 tbsp / 40 g / 1½ oz hard white cooking fat
1 egg yolk
few drops water
Filling
1 large or 3 medium tomatoes, skinned
few leaves of basil, chopped or ½ tsp dried basil
¾ cup / 100 g / 4 oz prawns, shrimps, crab or lobster meat, fresh or canned
3 eggs
⅝ cup / 150 ml / ¼ pt double or whipping cream
salt and freshly ground white pepper
Oven temperature 200°C / 400°F / Gas 6 reducing to 170°C / 325°F / Gas 3

1 Make up the pastry by sieving the flour into a bowl with the salt and add the fat to the flour in small pea-sized pieces. Rub in the fat until the mixture resembles fine breadcrumbs. Make a well in the centre of the mixture and add the egg yolk and 2–3 drops of water. Mix with a spatula and if it appears too dry, add a further 2 or 3 drops of water gradually (remember you can always add but not take out if the pastry is too wet). Knead lightly with your hand and the bowl should be clean and the pastry a firm smooth dough. Rest in the fridge for about 20 minutes.

2 Meanwhile prepare an 18-cm / 8-in flan ring (pie plate) on a baking sheet or use a china quiche dish. Cut a piece of greaseproof (waxed) paper slightly larger than the dish and have some dried beans such as kidney or haricot which can be kept for baking pastry ready for use.

3 Lightly flour the work top and roll out the pastry to fit the dish about ½ cm / ¼ in thick and about 4 cm / ½ in bigger than the quiche. Lift the pastry on the rolling pin and ease onto the dish. Run the rolling pin over the top of the dish to remove the pastry evenly.

4 Line with paper and baking beans and bake for 20 minutes. Reduce heat after quiche is removed from the oven.

5 Slice the tomatoes, place on the bottom of the flan case and sprinkle with basil. Spread the shellfish over the tomatoes.

6 Mix the eggs with the cream, season and pour into the prepared dish.

7 Return to the middle shelf in the oven until set and pale golden. Garnish with fresh watercress.

Alternatively make in individual tart pans for a first course or snack meal.

SMOKED SALMON QUICHE

Substitute 100 g / 4 oz chopped smoked salmon pieces for shellfish. Asparagus may be used in place of tomato. Omit basil.

Serves 4
4 tbsp vegetable oil
4 tbsp/50 g/2 oz butter
1 onion, peeled and finely chopped
2 spring (green) onions, washed and chopped
1 clove garlic, crushed
6 tomatoes, peeled and chopped or 1 × 400-g/14-oz can tomatoes
1 red pepper, deseeded and 1 green pepper, deseeded
1 bouquet garni
salt and freshly ground pepper
4 tbsp white wine
1 kg/2 lb squid, cleaned
2 tbsp brandy
2 cups/400 g/14 oz rice, cooked
½ tsp paprika
Oven temperature 180°C/350°F/Gas 4

1 Heat half the butter and oil in a frying pan and cook the onion, spring onion and crushed garlic for 4 minutes over a low heat.

2 Cut the peppers into strips and retain a few for garnish, add remainder to onion and cook for a further 2 minutes. Add the carrot, tomatoes, bouquet garni, and white wine. Season well and cook over a low heat for 5 minutes.

3 Cut the cleaned squid into even-sized pieces. Heat remaining oil and butter in a separate pan, cook the squid on a fairly high heat until golden. Heat the brandy in a ladle and ignite, pour over the squid when flames die away and add the squid to the vegetable mixture and cook, covered, in the oven for 20-25 minutes.

4 Meanwhile oil a ring mould of 20-25 cm (8-10 in) and place the cooked rice in the mould, cover with foil and heat through in the oven, with the squid for 10-15 minutes.

5 Unmould the rice in a heated serving dish, fill with the squid mixture and garnish with strips of peppers.

Smoked salmon quiche

DRESSED CRAB

Serves 2

1 crab, cooked
2 tbsp white breadcrumbs
1–2 tbsp Mayonnaise (see p 22)
½ tsp French mustard
salt and freshly ground pepper
juice of ½ lemon

To garnish

fresh parsley, finely chopped
paprika pepper
1 egg, hard-boiled (hard-cooked)
lettuce

1 Place the cooked crab on a board and twist the claws until they separate from the body. Crack the claws open with a hammer. Take a skewer and remove the white meat from the claws and place in a bowl.

2 Take hold of the crab firmly with two hands and with the thumbs push the body section away from the shell.

3 Take out and discard the following: the small sac or stomach bag which is attached to the large shell, any green tinged material in the large shell and, lastly, the grey spongy parts known as 'dead man's fingers'.

4 Scrape the brownish meat from the shell into a second bowl.

5 Cut the body into two and scrape any white meat left into the first bowl.

6 Tap the shell to remove the ragged sharp edge. Wash and scrub the inside and outside of the shell thoroughly and rinse well (do not use soap).

7 Dry off the shell and brush with some olive oil.

8 Mix the white breadcrumbs with the brown meat and cream well with the mayonnaise, French mustard and seasonings.

9 Arrange the white meat mixed with lemon juice and salt and pepper on each side of the shell and the brown meat down the middle.

10 Garnish with rows of chopped parsley, paprika and the separately sieved white and yolk of egg.

Arrange by placing the garnish on the edge of the spatula. Serve on a bed of lettuce surrounded by small claws, with thinly sliced wholewheat bread and butter. Serve mayonnaise separately.

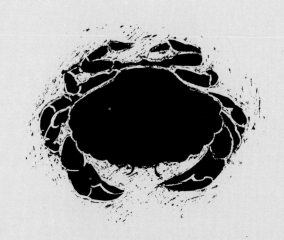

Serves 4 as a starter
24 large prawns or shrimps, cooked
bunch of parsley or watercress

1 Arrange the prawns or shrimps with the tails over the rim of a large glass goblet.

2 Stand on a glass plate and make a garland with the remaining prawns or shrimps and parsley or watercress round the plate.

Serve with Mayonnaise or Aïoli (see p 22).

Serves 4
2 small potatoes, peeled and thinly sliced
1 onion, peeled and finely chopped
2 cloves garlic, crushed
1–2 tbsp oil
2 tbsp curry powder
1½ cups / 1 × 425-g / 15-oz can tomatoes
1 tbsp tomato purée (paste)
300 ml / ½ pt fish stock or water
3 cups / 175 g / 6 oz small mushrooms
bay leaf
1 bouquet garni
½ cauliflower, washed and broken into florets
2¼ cups / 350 g / 12 oz prawns or shrimps
1 tbsp lemon juice
salt and freshly ground pepper
1⅓ cups / 250 g / 8 oz long grain rice, cooked

1 Parboil potatoes for 3 minutes. Drain and set aside.

2 Sauté the onion and garlic in the oil for several minutes until the onion is transparent.

3 Add the curry powder and fry mixing with the onions for a few minutes.

4 Add the tomatoes, purée and fish stock or water and chopped mushroom stalks. Add herbs. Bring to the boil, then lower heat.

5 Add the parboiled potatoes, the cauliflower and the whole mushrooms to the mixture and simmer for 25 minutes.

Add the cooked prawns or shrimps and lemon juice and simmer for a further 10 minutes on a low heat. Season to taste.

Serve on a bed of cooked rice with poppadums and chutneys.

SCALLOPS

SCALLOPS

The scallop is a bivalve shellfish which is easily
recognized by the familiar fan-shaped shell.   It is
also well known by its French name, Coquille Saint-
Jacques.

It is useful to obtain the shells when buying scallops as
they are ideal for serving scallop recipes. The fish
shop will prepare the scallops by removing the
inedible parts and the beards. However, if you are
using the shells to serve the fish, remove the scallops
and scrub the shells inside and out with a stiff brush to
remove all traces of shell crust. Do not use soap but
rinse well in cold water, after scrubbing. To re-use the
shells, it is advisable to clean well and bring to the boil
in a saucepan of water and then allow to dry and store
in a plastic bag.

SCALLOPS AU GRATIN

Serves 4
8–16 scallops, depending on size
2–4 tbsp / 25–50 g / 1–2 oz butter
1 small onion, peeled and finely chopped or 6 spring (green) onions, cleaned and chopped
1 clove garlic, crushed (optional)
⅝ cup / 150 ml / ¼ pt white wine
⅝ cup / 150 ml / ¼ pt fish stock or water
1 bay leaf
1 bouquet garni
salt and freshly ground pepper
1½ tbsp / 20 g / ¾ oz butter
3 tbsp / 20 g / ¾ oz flour
1–2 tbsp single (cereal) cream
2 tbsp fresh breadcrumbs, dried
1 tbsp parmesan cheese

1 Cut the scallops into slices. Melt the butter in a saucepan.

2 Sweat the onion and garlic over a low heat for about 3 minutes.

3 Add the sliced scallops, cook for a further 1 minute and then add the wine and water or fish stock with the bay leaf and bouquet garni. Season well.

4 Bring to the boil and turn the heat down low and simmer for about 6 minutes. Allow to cool.

5 Strain the liquor from the scallops, retaining the vegetables. Discard the bay leaf and bouquet garni.

6 Pipe a border of mashed potatoes around 8 deep, cleaned scallop shells.

7 Make a roux with the butter and flour, make a sauce with the fish liquor. Taste for seasoning, add cream.

8 Add the onion mixture, then the scallops to the sauce and divide the mixture between the shells.

9 Sprinkle with a mixture of breadcrumbs and parmesan cheese. Brown in a hot oven or under the grill (broiler).

If using 8 scallops, you will only need 4 shells and 1 tbsp cream. One shell is sufficient for a fish course but 2 will be needed for a main course.

SCALLOPS WITH MUSHROOMS

Serves 4
⅝ cup / 150 ml / ¼ pt dry white wine
⅝ cup / 150 ml / ¼ pt water
1 small onion, peeled and sliced
4 peppercorns
1 bay leaf
1 stalk parsley
1¾ cups / 100 g / 4 oz mushrooms, washed
4 tbsp / 50 g / 2 oz butter
1 medium onion, peeled and finely chopped or 8 spring (green) onions, washed and chopped
2 tomatoes, skinned and chopped
8 scallops, cleaned
3 tbsp / 20 g / ¾ oz flour
1 egg yolk
1 tbsp single (cereal) cream
few drops of lemon juice
2 tbsp fresh breadcrumbs, dried
To garnish
lemon wedges
parsley
Oven temperature 180°C / 350°F / Gas 4

1 Place the first six ingredients in a saucepan, bring to the boil and simmer for about 10 minutes.

2 Remove the mushroom stalks and chop finely. Slice the caps, retaining 16 slices for garnish.

3 Melt 2 tbsp / 25 g / 1 oz butter in a frying pan and sweat the chopped onion or spring onions and chopped mushroom stalks over a low heat for about 4 minutes. Add the tomatoes and cook for 3 minutes.

4 Add the sliced scallops to the strained wine mixture and poach over a low heat for about 8 minutes. Remove the scallops with a slotted spoon and then poach the mushroom slices for about 2 minutes. Strain the liquid into a measuring jug and make up to 1¼ cups / 300 ml / ½ pt, if necessary, with wine or water.

5 Make a roux with the remaining butter and flour and make into a sauce with the fish liquor. Allow to cool slightly then add a little sauce to the egg yolk, mix well and return the mixture to the sauce. Stir over a low heat for about 1 minute. Allow to cool slightly, add the cream and, lastly, the sliced mushrooms.

6 Divide the onion, mushroom and tomato mixture between the shells or spread on the bottom of the serving dish if using one big dish.

7 Add the scallops to the mushroom sauce, taste for seasoning and add a few drops of lemon juice to taste. Pour into the shells or serving dish and sprinkle with crumbs and garnish with mushrooms. Heat through in the oven for 10–15 minutes.

Milk may be substituted for wine, if liked.

Garnish with parsley and lemon wedges.

CURRIED SCALLOPS

Add 1 tsp curry powder to the onion and tomato mixture and fry for about 1 minute over a high heat. Add the mixture to the sauce. Water or fish stock may be used in place of wine for the curry. Serve with lemon wedges.

Serves 4
450 g / 1 lb cod or halibut
2½ cups / 600 ml / 1 pt Court-Bouillon (see p 19)
4 tbsp oil
2 cloves garlic, crushed
3 medium onions, peeled
1¾ cups / 350 g / 12 oz long grain rice
pinch of saffron or ¼ tsp turmeric
2½ cups / 600 ml / 1 pt fish or chicken stock
1 red pepper, deseeded
1 green pepper, deseeded
⅝ cup / 150 ml / ¼ pt white wine and water
650 g / 1½ pt mussels
generous cup / 175 g / 6 oz peeled prawns or shrimps
To garnish
wedges of lemon
1 tbsp parsley, chopped
4–8 large cooked prawns or shrimps (optional)

1 Poach the cod in 600 ml / 1 pt court-bouillon for 5 minutes.

2 Put the oil in a large pan and sweat the garlic and 2 of the onions, one thinly sliced and the other finely chopped, for about 4 minutes without browning.

3 Add the rice to the pan and stir over the heat for a few minutes until rice just begins to colour.

4 Strain the cod and retain the stock. Add saffron or turmeric to the stock and pour over the rice, stirring from time to time over a low heat. Cook covered with a lid or foil for the first 10 minutes.

5 Blanch the peppers for 2 minutes then dice finely, add to the rice and stir well.

6 In another saucepan, place the other finely chopped onion with water and wine mixture and a good shake of pepper. Bring to the boil and add the cleaned mussels. Cook for 10 minutes until steamed open.

7 Add the strained mussel liquor to the rice and stir well. Cook for a further 5 minutes or until tender.

8 Add chunks of white fish, prawns or shrimps and mussels.

Serve piping hot sprinkled with parsley and garnished with lemon wedges.

STUFFED COURGETTES (ZUCCHINI)

Serves 2–4
4 courgettes (zucchini)
¾ cup / 100 g / 4 oz prawns or shrimps
1 hard-boiled (hard-cooked) egg
1¼ cups / 300 ml / ½ pt Béchamel Sauce (see p 18)
1 tbsp parmesan cheese, grated
Oven temperature 180°C / 350°F / Gas 4

1 Cut a small slice lengthwise along the courgettes and scoop out a little of the flesh. Chop finely.

2 Blanch for 2 minutes in boilng salted water.

3 Add the prawns or shrimps, chopped egg and chopped courgette to the béchamel sauce.

4 Fill the courgettes with the mixture and sprinkle with parmesan cheese. Bake in the oven for 15–20 minutes.

This mixture can also be used to fill 2 blanched peppers.

SHELLFISH BISQUE

Serves 4
24 large prawns or shrimps
2 tbsp / 25 g / 1 oz butter
1 medium onion, peeled and diced
1 carrot, peeled and diced
sprig of thyme or ¼ tsp dried thyme
1 bay leaf
1 bouquet garni
3 stalks parsley
2 tbsp brandy
4 tbsp white wine
4¼ cups / 1 l / 1¾ pt water or fish stock
2 tbsp / 25 g / 1 oz butter
4 tbsp / 25 g / 1 oz flour
salt and freshly ground pepper
4 tbsp cream

1 Wash the prawns thoroughly. Remove the shells and retain both shells and prawns or shrimps separately. Crush the shells in a plastic bag with a rolling pin.

2 Melt the butter in a saucepan and sweat the onions and carrots over a low heat for about 5 minutes, then add 8 prawns or shrimps.

3 Add thyme, bay leaf, bouquet garni and parsley at the side of the pan.

4 Pour the brandy into a ladle and heat, set alight and pour over the shellfish and vegetables. Add the white wine and simmer for 2 minutes.

5 Pour the stock into the saucepan and add the crushed prawn shells. Bring to the boil and simmer for 35 minutes.

6 Mix the butter and flour together with the fingertips into a paste and form into small balls.

7 Pass the soup through a fine sieve. Return soup to the saucepan, and stirring over a low heat add the balls of flour and butter until the mixture has thickened. Taste for seasoning and add the rest of the prawns for the last 5 minutes cooking time. Stir in the cream just before serving.

VARIATION

Lobster or crayfish shells may be crushed, brought to the boil and simmered with the vegetables. Continue to make soup as in method given above. If the lobster meat has already been eaten, canned lobster may be used as a garnish or the soup may be served without meat.

Stuffed courgettes (zucchini)